Design and Make Food in the Pri[mary School]

Adrienne Dawes

Introduction

Many children will have enjoyed baking activities before entering school, either at Nursery, Play school or home. Food is an essential part of all our lives and the use of food as a material area in Design Technology harnesses the pupils enthusiasm and enables activities to be carried out that involve the sensory experiences of sight, touch, taste and smell.

No matter what experiences of cutting, shaping, measuring and mixing food ingredients the pupils have, the challenge of creating a recipe of their own after tasting a variety of ingredients is an exciting and rewarding use of their skills. Opportunities to involve food activities during Design Technology occur many times throughout the school year. Festivals, celebrations and a variety of topics provide children with a real purpose for their work.

Once the basic skills have been introduced, then the pupils own creativity can be left to flourish. When the basic techniques have been introduced to the pupils and they have been given time to experiment with a range of ingredients, then the teacher must ensure that:-

- Health and Safety guidelines are adhered to.
- The project / task given to the pupils is demanding enough to allow them to perform at a higher level.
- The task is interesting so that the pupils are encouraged to persist.
- A variety of equipment is available to ensure appropriate choices can be made.
- All equipment and materials are available in the class and they are easily accessible so as to ensure pupils make the correct decisions.
- Sufficient time is allowed to enable thorough experimentation by individuals, that they can practice newly acquired skills, be taught how to correctly use any new pieces of equipment, develop ideas and apply finishing techniques.
- The teacher needs to have the skills and knowledge necessary to intervene when appropriate.

Experimentation and choice on the part of the pupil is very important. This book contains photocopiable resources and teacher / pupil instructions which will enable you to teach and practise a variety of skills and techniques appropriate to a variety of food activities. The activities are designed to assist adults when introducing new techniques to Key Stage one and Key Stage two pupils and when used by a whole school will ensure progression.

The activities are intended to be used as an introduction and when the pupils have completed these introductory activities they should be provided with a range of materials and equipment to enable them to create their own recipe / food items suitable for a given theme, occasion or individuals needs.

Contents

Background information 2

Key Stage 1 Recipes
Icing Sugar Sweets 6
Colourful Heart Biscuits 8
Jellies 10
Coleslaw 12
Gingerbread Men 14
Christmas Gingerbreads 16
Decorated Buns 18
Sandwich 20
Healthy Salad 22
Chocolate Easter Nest 24
Five Fruit Salad 26
Layered Ice Lolly 28
Cordial Cocktails 30
Flavoured Milk Shakes 32
Weights and Measures 35

Key Stage 1 Recipes
Spiced Biscuits 36
Pancakes 38
Bread and Butter pudding 40
Meringues 42
Bread 44
Chapatti 46
Pizza Base 48
Pizza Topping 50
Jacket Potato 52
Omelette 54
Christmas Cake 56
Additional Recipes 58
Food Packaging 62

Other Design & Make books in the series are available from all good Educational Bookshops and by mail order from:

**Topical Resources, P.O. Box 329,
Broughton, Preston, Lancashire. PR3 5LT**

Topical Resources publishes a range of Educational Materials for use in Primary Schools and Pre-School Nurseries and Playgroups.

For the latest catalogue:
Tel: **01772 863158** *Fax:* **01772 866153**
e.mail: **sales@topical-resources.co.uk**
or visit our Website at: **www.topical-resources.co.uk**

Copyright © 2000 Adrienne Dawes

Printed in Great Britain for "Topical Resources", Publishers of Educational Materials, P.O. Box 329, Broughton, Preston, Lancashire PR3 5LT by T.Snape & Company Limited, Boltons Court, Preston Lancashire.

Typeset by Paul Sealey Illustration & Design, 3 Wentworth Drive, Thornton, Lancashire.

First Published September 2000.
ISBN 1 872977 56 1

Practical Skills Involved in Food Activities

All of these skills are applicable for any pupil at any age or level. It is the teacher's expectations, the materials, the resources provided and the development of the initial technique that will vary from stage to stage so that continuity and progression will be achieved.

Measuring and Marking
The pupils should measure the dry and wet ingredients used in their food work. A variety of equipment must be introduced to the pupils to enable them at a later stage to make choices as to the most appropriate for a given task.

Dry Measurement	Liquid Measurement
cups	cups
spoons	spoons
balance scales	measuring jugs
spring balance scales	
electronic scales	
grams & milligrams	**litres and millilitres**

It is important to record the amounts of ingredients added to any recipe so that if successful the product can be made again or adjustments can be made.

Cutting and Shaping
A wide variety of equipment should be made available to the pupils, however care should be taken when using sharp knives and part of the schools health and safety guidelines should address this issue.

The pupils should be given the opportunity to tear, slice, dice, shread, chop and grate foodstuffs. The design brief should be referred to:
e.g. Fruit salad pieces are not too large to be eaten with a spoon.
Biscuits are easy to hold and not so large that they break easily.
Sandwiches can be handled easily.

Cutting and Shaping Equipment: a variety of knives, graters, pastry cutters, rolling pins

Joining and Combining
Before the pupils can make decisions as to which ingredients should be combined in a recipe, they should taste and evaluate a variety of foodstuffs appropriate to the given task. Decisions about the recipe should be made when considering the design brief. Is the food to be made for personal preferences or for other people, in which case a survey would need to be carried out.

A variety of equipment should be introduced to the pupils so that they can make appropriate choices when combining ingredients.

Joining and Combining Equipment: sieve, hand whisk, rotary whisk, fork, a variety of spoons, bowls in a variety of sizes etc.

Decorating and Finishing
The pupils need to recognise the importance of the presentation of foodstuffs. When the finished products are presented they should be aesthetically pleasing:
eg - fruit salad should be a mixture of colour and carefully cut pieces.
- buns and cakes may need icing or additional decoration.
- biscuits should be cut/shaped and a certain degree of consistency maintained.

During the activities the pupils will be involved in:-
- Observing
- Evaluating - an ongoing process which will involve investigating and disassembling simple teacher prepared and manufactured food items.
- Exploring and Investigating - the pupils should choose ingredients after investigating their properties eg taste, colour; and relate these to the suitability of the ingredients for the making task.
- Organising and planning - resources need to be organised to allow pupils to select for themselves.
- Testing - could it taste / look better? Does it do what was intended? What do others think about it?
- Explaining and communicating - the pupils should be encouraged to talk as a means of recording what they have done, or are intending to do.
- Designing and Making - this book contains photocopiable sheets to enable new skills to be introduced which can then be developed and practiced in a variety of situations in the primary school. At a later stage the pupils should be provided with a range of materials and tools to enable them to develop the skill further. They should be allowed time to develop and refine the introduced technique and be taught the importance of consistency and quality.

Teacher Preparation

It is very important that before undertaking any activity involving food the adults and pupils involved are aware of the school's Health and Safety guidelines.

The teacher must ensure that:-

- Adults are aware of any dietary restrictions/requirements that influence children in the group/ class.

- Parents / guardians are informed that a food activity will take place.

- Hands should be washed and wiped on paper towels.

- Tables should be covered with plastic cloths that are used only for food work.

- Plastic cloths should be wiped with disposable cloths and a steriliser e.g. Dettox.

- Aprons should be worn.

- All equipment used should be stored in a covered box or suitable cupboard and the equipment should be used only for food work.

- No glass or wooden equipment should be used.

- Perishable food is stored in a fridge and sell by dates should be adhered to.

- Care should be taken with • ovens • sharp knives

- All equipment should be washed after use, using water which is as hot as possible.

- Equipment should be washed in a bowl used only for food work.

- Equipment should be dried with paper towels and stored away.

- Any food items taken home should be carried in plastic bags.

Key Stage 1

It is important that young children are given the opportunity to learn through doing, talking and problem solving.
Food activities are an ideal way to help pupils to be involved in an exciting and rewarding activity which will help them develop personal qualities such as co-operation and creativity.

The activities in which the pupils are involved should be relevant, realistic and challenging and should also be enjoyable.

Pupils should be given the opportunity to:
- develop their knowledge and understanding of safe and hygienic working conditions and practices when working with food.

- develop an awareness that foods have different tastes and textures.

- develop appropriate vocabulary to describe different tastes and textures.

- develop an awareness that people prefer different tastes / foods and that factors such as family and cultural experiences influence their preferences.

- follow instructions from a recipe.

- develop practical skills:
  Measuring / Marking - using non standard measurements eg spoons, cups, drops etc...
  following a recipe using grams and mls (equipment - teaspoons, cups, tablespoons, paintbrushes, weighing scales, plastic measuring jugs)

  Cutting / Shaping - sweets, dicing fruit, moulding bread (equipment - sweet and biscuit cutters, rolling pins, plastic knives)

  Joining / Combining - mixing dry and dry ingredients together, mixing liquid and liquid ingredients together, mixing dry and liquid ingredients together. (equipment - spoons, bowls, whisks, forks)

- understand the aesthetics concerning food presentation, develop the practical skills associated with Finishing and Decorating.

Food activities should be linked in a meaningful way with Science activities in the Key Stage 1 class and it is therefore important to provide the pupils with some basic information on the food cycle and nutrition either before or during the design and technology activity as the knowledge gained will help the pupils make informed choices about the ingredients used.

Background Information for Key Stage 1 Pupils

We all have favourite foods but food is more important than just something to eat, we need food to live - our bodies need food. Food is the fuel which supplies energy to keep our bodies working and it is also needed to build a strong and healthy body. Food gives us the energy to live. The body must have a variety of different foods if it is to be healthy.

All living things depend on food to stay alive and the food chain is dependent upon green plants as can be seen from this food cycle diagram:

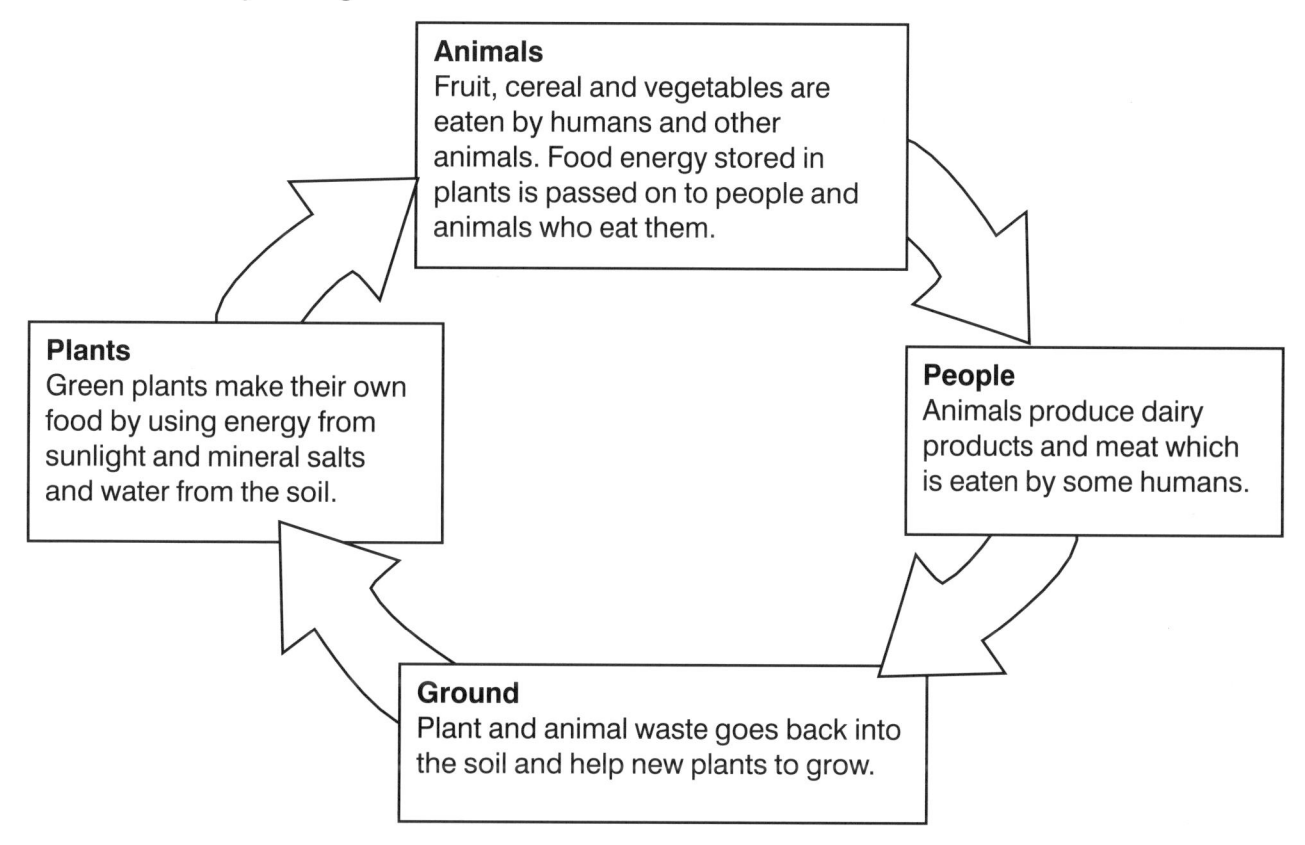

Animals
Fruit, cereal and vegetables are eaten by humans and other animals. Food energy stored in plants is passed on to people and animals who eat them.

Plants
Green plants make their own food by using energy from sunlight and mineral salts and water from the soil.

People
Animals produce dairy products and meat which is eaten by some humans.

Ground
Plant and animal waste goes back into the soil and help new plants to grow.

Nutrients and liquids from food are absorbed into the body when the foods are eaten.
Some foods are eaten raw, other foods are better to eat after they have been cooked.
Cooking can improve the -   flavour
texture
appearance
colour

Think about some foods which you like to eat. Describe what they are like raw and what they are like when they have been cooked. You could try cheese, meat, vegetables and fruit.

Foods can be cooked in different ways:
- Boiling   in boiling water on the cooker top.
- Frying   in shallow / deep oil on the cooker top.
- Steaming   in steam from a pan of boiling water.
- Baking   in dry heat from the oven.

Which foods are baked, fried, boiled or steamed? Make a list.

Icing Sugar Sweets

Equipment needed:
- mixing bowl
- cups
- tablespoon
- fork
- teaspoon
- small cutters
- plates
- paintbrushes
- rolling pin

Ingredients:
- 2 cups of icing sugar
- water
- flavourings eg mint, vanilla, lemon etc.
- food colourings eg red, blue, yellow, green etc.

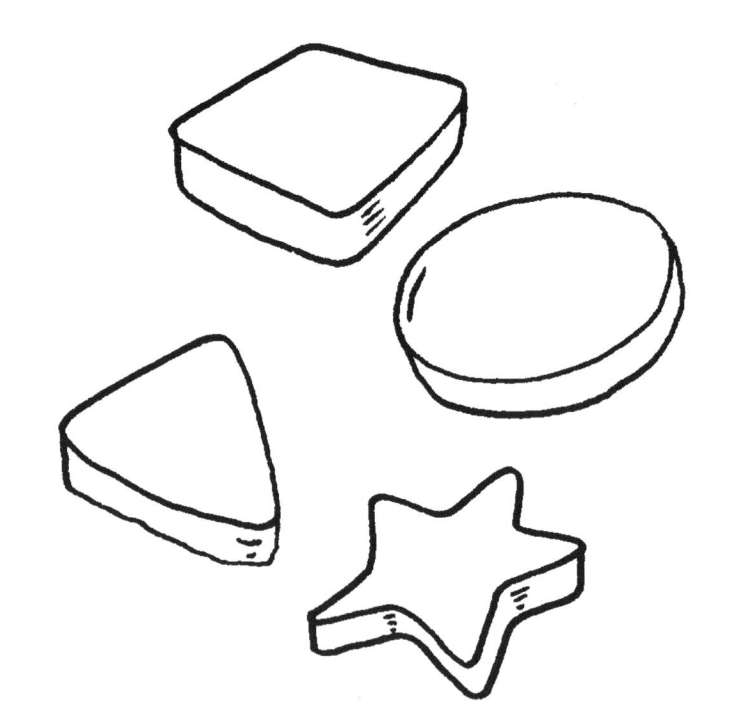

The Process:

Step 1. Place two cups of icing sugar into a bowl.
Step 2. Add one tablespoon of water and mix with a fork.
Step 3. Add one drop of flavouring using a clean paintbrush.
Step 4. Add one drop of colouring using a clean paintbrush.
Step 5. Mix together and add more water to the mixture if needed, one teaspoon at a time until you have a thick paste.
Step 6. Taste the mixture and evaluate. Add more flavouring if required.
Step 7. Look at the mixture and evaluate the appearance. Add more colouring if required.
Step 8. Roll out, cut and shape the sweets.
Step 9. Display the finished sweets on a plate and allow the pupils to evaluate each others.
Step 10. It is important that the pupils clear away and wash the equipment in soapy water which is as hot as is safe.
Step 11. Photocopy the sheet opposite, one per child, colour and complete the pictures and sentences.

How the idea may be developed:

The pupils could work in groups and evaluate the flavourings before using them in their recipe.
The sweets can be rolled into balls and pressed into flat shapes if small cutters are not available.
The finished sweets could be sprinkled with icing sugar or have small jellied sweets pressed into the top of them.
Different shapes of cutters could be used for different festivals eg At Christmas the pupils could create stars, trees, bells etc.

Name _____

How to Make Icing Sugar Sweets

I wore an _____

I washed my _____

The table was covered with a _____

____ drops of flavouring

____ drops of colouring

____ cups of icing sugar

| My sweets looked like this: | They tasted of: _____ _____ _____ |

Colourful Heart Biscuits

Equipment needed:
    teaspoon
    mixing spoon
    weighing scales
    baking tray
    rolling pin
    sieve
    oven gloves
    heart shaped cutters
    2 mixing bowls
    circle biscuit cutter
    greaseproof paper
    oven
    plastic cup

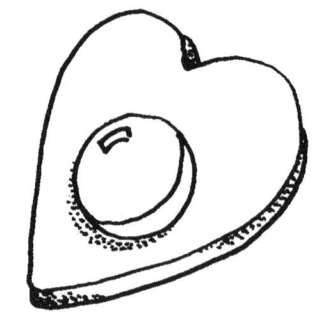

Ingredients:
    240 grams flour
    120 grams sugar
    pinch of salt
    120 grams margarine
    quarter of a teaspoon of baking powder
    half an egg
    Fox's Glacier fruit sweets (or similar boiled sweets)

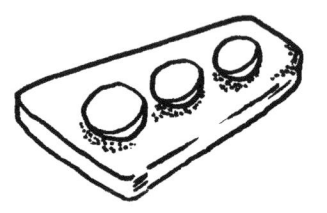

The Process:
Step 1.   The pupils, working in groups under adult supervision should weigh out the ingredients prior to combining them.
Step 2.   Sieve the flour, salt and baking powder together in a mixing bowl.
Step 3.   Cream the sugar and fat together in a large mixing bowl.
Step 4.   Add the half of a beaten egg.
Step 5.   Stir the flour mixture into the large mixing bowl and mix with a plastic spoon.
Step 6.   Place the mixture onto a floured surface and use a floured rolling pin to roll the mixture out thinly.
Step 7.   Use the heart shaped cutter to cut out the biscuit shape and use the smaller circle cutter to make a hole in the centre of the heart. Place the pupil's choice of boiled sweet in the centre hole.
Step 8.   Place the biscuit shapes onto greaseproof paper on a baking tray and place into a pre-heated oven at 175 degrees celsius.
Step 9.   Bake for 15 - 20 minutes until brown.
Step 10.   An adult should remove the biscuits from the oven and allow to cool before removing from the baking tray. Take Care! - The melted sweets are very hot!
Step 11.   Photocopy the sheet opposite, one per child and complete.

How the idea may be developed:
The children could use different shaped cutters to create their biscuits.
Traffic light biscuits could be made using red, orange and green glacier fruits.
The colourful biscuits can be used as christmas tree decorations by making a hole for the ribbon before baking.
Ready mixed Icing sugar from tubes could be added to the biscuits as further decoration.
Investigate whether or not glacier mints could be used.

Name _____

Colourful Heart Biscuits

This is how my finished biscuit looked:

We used a recipe to make _____.

We had to weigh the _____ carefully.

We put a _____ in the middle of the biscuits.

We had to take care with the hot _____ and the hot _____.

Jellies

Equipment needed:
　　jelly moulds
　　kettle
　　measuring jugs
　　spoons

Ingredients:
　　a variety of coloured jellies

The Process:
Step 1.　　Photocopy the sheet opposite, one per child. Discuss with the pupils the order in which they think the jellies should be made.
Step 2.　　Cut out the sequence pictures and arrange them in the correct order.
Step 3.　　Make the jellies.
Step 4.　　Break the jellies into pieces in a heatproof measuring jug.
Step 5.　　Boil the kettle and the supervising adult should add the water to the measuring jug according to the instructions.
Step 6.　　Stir the mixture until the jelly pieces have melted.
Step 7.　　Pour the melted jelly into the moulds. If the mixture is allowed to cool then small yogurt pots can be used which would be more suitable for evaluating purposes.
Step 8.　　Place 1 jelly into the fridge and the other should be left in a cool area in the classroom.
Step 9.　　Leave the jellies for approximately 2 hours and compare them. What has happened to the jelly in the fridge? What has happened to the jelly in the classroom?
Step 10.　　Let the pupils taste the set jellies. Place the unset jelly into the fridge to set.
Step 11.　　Allow the pupils to stick the photocopied pictures in their correct order. Display with the process.

How the idea may be developed:
This activity could be linked with Science work.
Chopped fruit or tinned fruit cocktail can be added to the jelly before it sets. The children could create a trifle by adding a variety of different ingredients:
eg　　fruit
　　　sponge biscuits
　　　custard
　　　cream
　　　additional decoration - cherries, chocolate drops, jellied sweets, hundreds and thousands etc.

Milk Jelly
Use half evaporated milk in place of half of the boiling water to mix the jelly pieces; however allow the jelly to melt in the boiling water and leave time for the water to cool before adding the evaporated milk or it will curdle. Does the addition of the evaporated milk affect the taste of the jelly? How does it affect the appearance of the jelly?
Compare the jellies. Which do the children prefer?

Name _____

How to Make Jellies

We stirred the jelly pieces until they had melted.

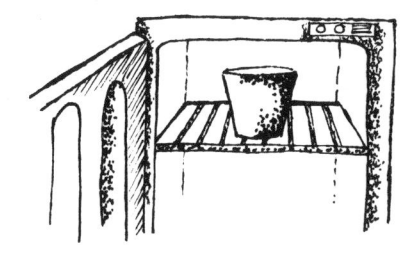

We placed one jelly in the fridge and left one in the classroom.

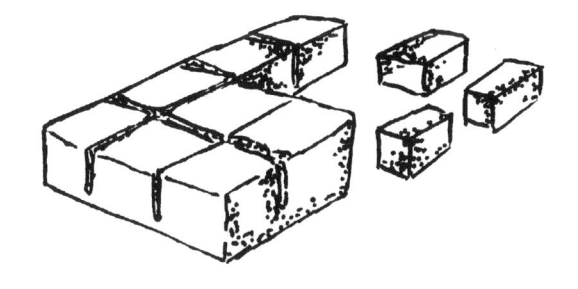

We broke the jelly into pieces.

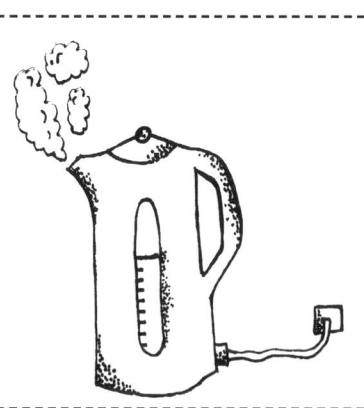

We boiled the kettle.

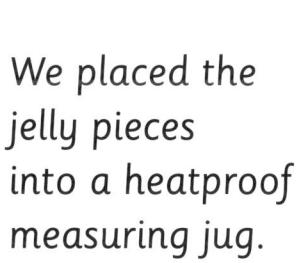

We placed the jelly pieces into a heatproof measuring jug.

We poured the boiling water over the jelly pieces.

We poured the jelly mixture into moulds.

We evaluated the set jellies.

This is a picture of my favourite jelly.

I liked this jelly because:

_____

_____

_____

_____

© Topical Resources. May be photocopied for classroom use only.   11

Coleslaw

An activity that will teach the pupils how to shred, chop, grate and slice various salad ingredients.

Equipment needed:
  chopping board
  mixing bowl
  spoon
  sharp knife for cutting and shreading
  grater

Ingredients:
  225 grams cabbage
  1 onion
  1 stick celery
  a quarter of a green pepper
  a quarter of a red pepper
  2 radishes
  a quarter of a cucumber
  1 apple
  1 large carrot
  salad cream

How to make the example:
Step 1. Wash the ingredients and dry with a paper towel.
Step 2. Use the sharp cutting knives with care! Chop and shred all of the ingredients into long thin pieces.
Step 3. Place all of the ingredients into a large mixing bowl and mix together thoroughly.
Step 4. Add the salad cream to the chopped ingredients one spoonful at a time and mix.
Step 5. When all the ingredients are coated with the salad cream then the coleslaw is ready.
Step 6. Taste the coleslaw and evaluate.
  Consider: Taste
    Texture
    Appearance

How the idea may be developed:
Allow the pupils to taste all the ingredients and decide which ones will be incorporated into their coleslaw.
Could the ingredients be grated? How would this effect the taste, texture and appearance of the finished product?
Evaluate manufactured coleslaw and compare it to the coleslaw made by the pupils.

What other ingredients could be used?
Try: beetroot
    spring onions
    apple etc..

What could the coleslaw be served with?

Name _____

How to Make Coleslaw

We have been taught how to chop, slice, grate and tear a variety of ingredients to make coleslaw.

For my coleslaw I chose the following ingredients and practiced a variety of skills using different pieces of equipment.

Ingredients: (eg. Radish)	Equipment used: (eg. knife and cutting board)	Method of preparation: (eg. slicing)

We evaluated the coleslaw using descriptive words. We considered:

Appearance: _____

Taste: _____

Texture: _____

Gingerbread Men

Gingerbread men with currant eyes and buttons appeal to children and are fun to make.
The activity can be linked to Literacy work by reading the story of 'The Gingerbread Man' to the class / group of pupils.
This recipe will make approximately 20 Gingerbread Men.

Equipment needed:
saucepan
weigh scales
spoons
sieve
rolling pin
Gingerbread man cutter
baking tray
oven gloves

Ingredients:
480g plain white flour
60g golden syrup
half teaspoon ground cinnamon
1 teaspoon bicarbonate of soda
currants

60g soft brown sugar
60g butter
half a teaspoon ground ginger
1 egg yolk

The Process:
Step 1.   Place the syrup, sugar and spices into a saucepan and heat gently until melted.
Step 2.   Stir in the butter and allow to melt.
Step 3.   Add the bicarbonate of soda and stir. Allow to cool.
Step 4.   Sieve the flour into a large mixing bowl and add the melted ingredients and the egg yolk.
Step 5.   Stir well to create a dough.
Step 6.   Place the dough onto a floured surface and knead lightly for 2 minutes.
Step 7.   Roll the dough out thinly on a floured surface and cut out the shapes using a Gingerbread Man cutter.
Step 8.   Decorate the shapes with currants and place onto a greased baking tray.
Step 9.   Bake in a pre heated oven (180 degrees celsius) for 20 - 30 minutes.
Step 10. Remove from the oven and allow to cool.
Step 11. Photocopy the sheet opposite, one per child and complete.

How the idea may be developed:
Animal figures could be created.

Sultanas and cherries could be used as decoration.

The pupils could experiment with the amount of spices added. Amounts added should be recorded and results from evaluations taken into consideration when baking further biscuits.

Name _____

My Gingerbread Man

Draw around the Gingerbread Man cutter and complete the picture to look like your finished biscuit.

Christmas Gingerbreads

Equipment needed:
- variety of shaped cutters
- rolling pin
- cooling rack
- oven
- weigh scales
- saucepan
- oven gloves
- baking tray

Ingredients:
- 200 grams self raising flour
- 50 grams soft margarine
- 50 grams soft brown sugar
- 2 level teaspoons ground ginger
- 1 level teaspoon ground cinnamon
- 2 heaped tablespoons golden syrup

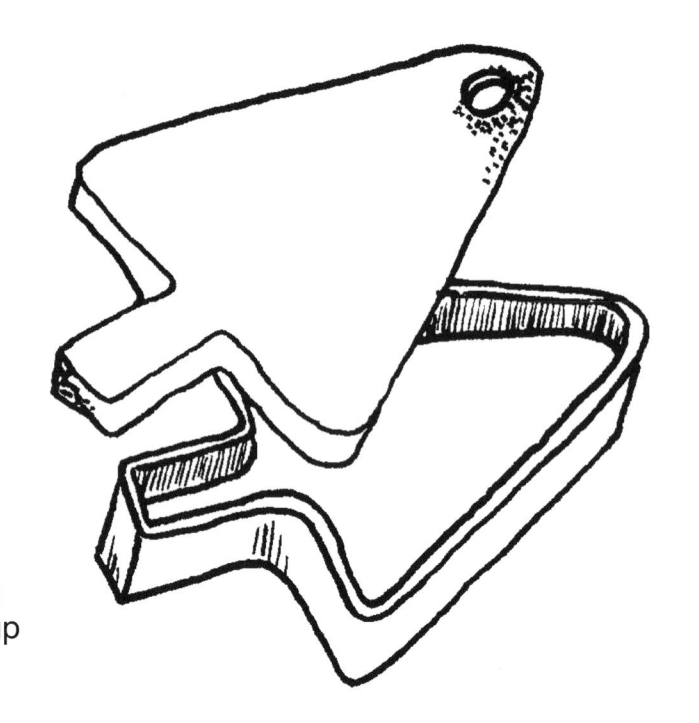

The Process:
Step 1.   Discuss with the pupils Christmas traditions in a variety of countries where the tradition is to decorate the Christmas Tree with gingerbread ornaments eg Scandinavia
Step 2.   In groups the children should weigh and measure the ingredients.
Step 3.   Photocopy the sheet opposite, one per child and follow the instructions in a group to create the gingerbread mixture.
Step 4.   Discuss with the children simple Christmas theme shapes eg bells, stars, Christmas trees, candles etc.
Step 5.   The children should either choose a manufactured shape or make a paper pattern and cut around this to create their biscuit shape.
Step 6.   Each child in the group should cut out 4 biscuit shapes and make holes at the top of them before baking. This hole is to place the ribbon through after baking.
Step 7.   Place the biscuits on a greased baking tray and bake in the oven set at 180 degrees celsius for 10 - 12 minutes until brown.
Step 8.   Place the biscuits on a tray to cool.
Step 9.   Thread ribbon through the holes in the top of the biscuits.
Step 10. Complete and colour the photocopied sheet.

How the idea may be developed:
The children could further decorate their gingerbread biscuits by:
- Icing them with white icing sugar (use ready made in tubes).
- Creating patterns on the biscuits with ready made coloured icing in tubes.
- Using icing sugar to stick jelly sweets, chocolate drops etc onto the biscuits.

Name _____

Gingerbread Biscuits

We turned the oven on and set it to 180 degrees centigrade.

We put the flour, cinnamon and ginger into a bowl and mixed them together. The margarine, sugar and syrup were placed in a saucepan and gentle heat was applied until they melted.

Everything was mixed together and then rolled into a ball. We sprinkled some flour onto the table covering and rolled out the gingerbread mixture. This is the shape I chose for my decoration:

When I had cut 4 shapes from the rolled out gingerbread mixture, I made holes in them and placed them on a baking tray. They were baked for_____ minutes and then allowed to cool.

My finished Christmas Gingerbread looked like this:

© Topical Resources. May be photocopied for classroom use only.

Decorated Buns

Equipment needed:
- large bowl
- 2 tablespoons
- bun tin
- paper bun cases
- weighing scales
- spatula
- small bowl
- table knife
- mixing spoon
- oven

Ingredients:

Bun
100 grams self raising flour
100 grams margarine
2 eggs
cherries
1 tablespoon water

Decoration
currants
chocolate drops
icing sugar
100 grams castor sugar
small sweets
dessicated coconut

The Process:

Step 1.   Weigh the ingredients prior to combining them.
Step 2.   Place the sugar and the margarine into a large bowl.
Step 3.   Place the 100 grams of self raising flour into the bowl.
Step 4.   Add the eggs and water to the ingredients and mix together.
Step 5.   When the ingredients are well mixed together and are a creamy consistency, spoon the mixture into paper bun cases which have been placed in a bun tin. The mixture will make 12 buns.
Step 6.   Place in the oven which is heated at 200 degrees celsius and cook for 10 - 15 minutes until golden brown.
Step 7.   Take out of the oven and leave to cool.
Step 8.   The pupils should be responsible for clearing away the equipment and washing up in soapy water which is as hot as they can stand. The equipment should then be stored away.
Step 9.   When the buns are cool, the children should decide on how they want to decorate them. This will depend upon the celebration / festival the buns are being made for, or the pupils imagination can be left to flourish and 'fantastic' buns can be created.
Step 10. It is important that the range of decoration ingredients are on show to encourage the pupils to make choices. Show the pupils how the icing sugar can be used as 'edible glue' to sick sweets etc onto the buns.
Step 11. Photocopy the sheet opposite, one per child and complete.

How the idea may be developed:
Cook half of the buns in the conventional oven and the other half in a microwave. How do the cooked buns differ?
Consider taste, cooking time and appearance.

Name _____

Making Buns

Draw pictures or write the ingredients used to make the buns.

I used:

Draw the equipment used:

The top of my bun looked like this when I had decorated it.

A Tasty Sandwich

Design and Make a sandwich that you would like to eat at a school party.
Consider taste, appearance and nutritional value.

Equipment needed:
    blunt knives for spreading
    sharp knives for cutting
    chopping board
    colander
    plates for presentation

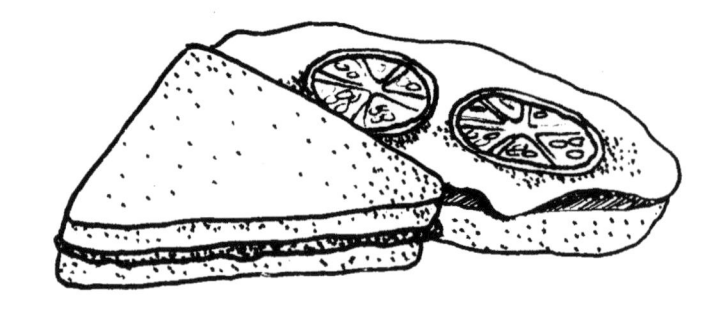

Ingredients:

white loaf	brown loaf	white baps
brown baps	margarine	jams
peanut butter	chocolate spread	cheese spread
cheese	salad cream	butter
tuna	a wide range of salad ingredients.	

The Process:
The children will be using the skills of spreading, chopping, cutting, grating and tearing depending on the ingredients they select. If the children have not been taught the skills during a previous activity then they should be taught before this activity takes place.

Step 1.   Discuss with the children their likes and dislikes. What sandwiches do they have for their packed lunches etc? Collect pictures of sandwiches from magazines. Try to visit a local bakery or supermarket to see what sandwiches they have for sale.

Step 2.   Let the pupils taste the range of breads that are available and any of the ingredients that they have not had before.

Step 3.   When the pupils have selected their bread, they should be taught how to spread the butter, cheese, salad cream or combination of the spreads that will 'stick' the ingredients into the sandwich.

Step 4.   Let the children create their sandwiches using as few or as many of the ingredients as they wish.

Step 5.   Photocopy the sheet opposite, one per child and complete. (This can be completed after or prior to the actual making.)

How the idea may be developed:
The sandwiches can be named by the children.
For Key Stage 2 pupils, the cost of the ingredients can be used to work out the cost of the sandwiches. What would the sandwiches have to be sold at to make a profit?
Discuss with the children the need for consistency if sandwiches are to be sold.

Name _____

What is in a Sandwich?

Draw the filling for your sandwich and label the ingredients.

Bread contains carbohydrates and fibre.
Carbohydrates give us energy.
Fibre helps to keep our digestive system working well.

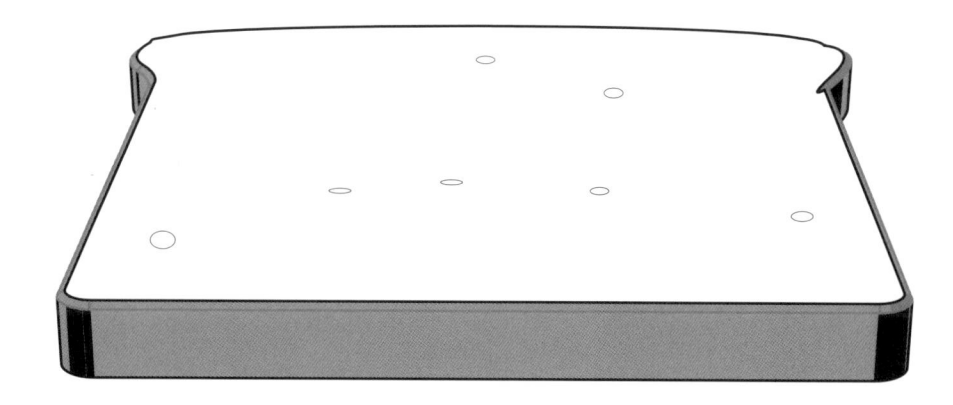

Butter contains fat, a principal source of energy.

Cheese contains protein, used to build strong and healthy bodies.

Salad contains vitamins and minerals.
Vitamin D in lettuce is for strong teeth, hair, nails and bones.

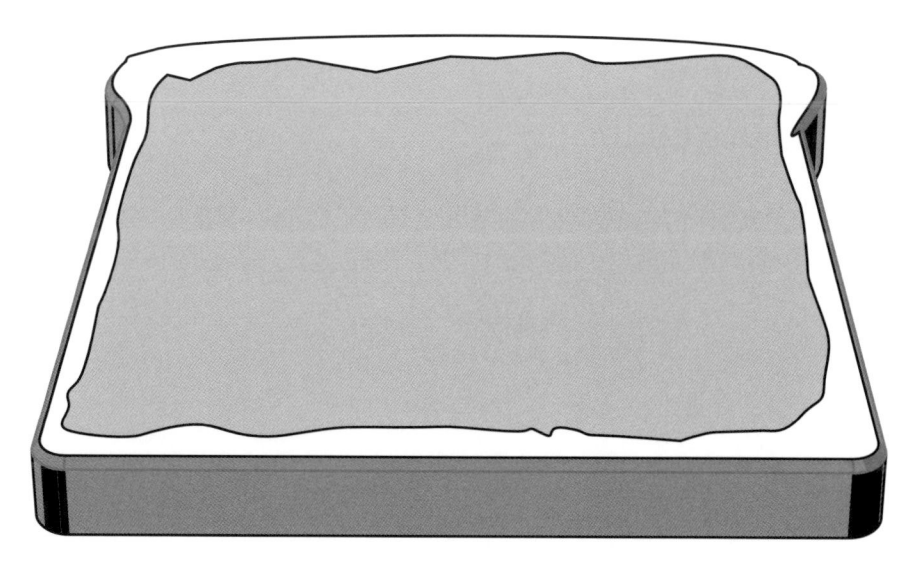

© Topical Resources. May be photocopied for classroom use only.

A Healthy Salad

Equipment needed:
- cutting board
- sharp knife
- plates
- bowls
- grater

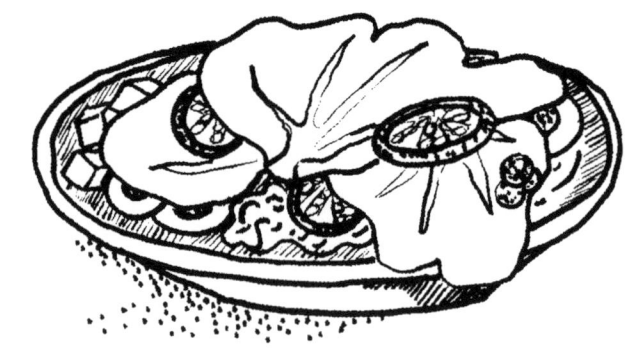

Ingredients:
- lettuce
- watercress
- tomatoes
- spring onions
- cress
- celery
- beetroot
- cabbage
- red pepper
- green pepper
- cucumber
- apples
- radish

How to make the example:
Step 1. Discuss the pupils likes and dislikes when they can see all of the ingredients.
Step 2. Let the pupils taste the ingredients that they have not had before.
Step 3. Ensure that the pupils can name all the ingredients. Create a display using pictures of the ingredients which are labelled.
Step 4. Ensure that all of the ingredients have been washed before the pupils begin to create their salad.
Step 5. Discuss with the pupils the different ways in which the ingredients can be prepared:
Lettuce & Watercress - tearing, chopping, shreading.
Cabbage - chopping, shreading, grating.
Peppers, Cucumber, Apples, Celery & Beetroot - chopping, dicing, grating.
Tomatoes, Spring Onions & Radish - whole, sliced.
Cress - cut with scissors.
Step 6. Photocopy the sheet opposite, one per pupil and complete the design task.
Step 7. The pupils should be given time to create their salad either in a bowl or on a plate.
Step 8. Evaluate the presentation of the salads.
Step 9. Evaluate the taste.

How the idea may be developed:
Salad sandwiches could be created.
What could the salad be served with? eg salad cream, coleslaw etc.
Discuss what meal would go well with salad? eg stuffed jacket potatoes, pizza etc.

Name _____

A Healthy Salad

I have chosen the following ingredients for my healthy salad and have also chosen the way in which it will be prepared.

Ingredients (eg cheese)	Equipment used (eg sharp knife)	Method of preparation (eg grating)

I hope my salad will look like this:

Chocolate Easter Nest

Equipment needed:
- a hob
- pan
- 2 mixing bowls
- water
- spoons
- paper bun cases

Ingredients:
- cornflakes
- rice crispies
- shredded wheat
- milk chocolate
- sugar and chocolate eggs

The Process:
Step 1. Let the pupils taste the cereals and record their preference on a graph.
Step 2. In groups the pupils should watch as an adult melts the chocolate in a bowl placed in a pan of boiling water. Discuss the safety aspects of this activity. Link to science work.
Step 3. Each pupil should be given a measured amount of their chosen cereal and a measured amount of melted milk chocolate.
Step 4. Mix the cereal into the chocolate and place into a paper bun case.
Step 5. Using a teaspoon form a nest shape in the bun case and allow to cool.
Step 6. When cool, a stated number of eggs should be placed into the chocolate nests. The pupils should choose between sugar and chocolate eggs after tasting.
Step 7. The pupils can either eat their nests at school or take them home in a small plastic bag for themselves or a relative/friend.
Step 8. Photocopy the sheet opposite, one per child and complete.

How the idea may be developed:
Increase the number of cereals that the pupils can choose from.
Increase the number of chocolates from which the pupils can choose after the tasting activity:
eg white chocolate - dark chocolate - orange chocolate etc.

Cooking chocolates are more cost effective but should be included in the tasting activity to see if the children select them.
Cereal biscuits can be created yet additional ingredients would need to be added
eg sultanas, raisins, dried banana, apricots, coconuts etc. chocolate pieces, honey, syrup etc..

N.B. If nuts are to be used extra care must be taken to ensure none of the pupils have food allergies.

Name _____

Design & Make a Chocolate Easter Nest

I tasted _____ cereals.
  (number of cereals)

I tasted _____
   _____
   _____
   (types of cereals)

I chose _____ for my Easter Nest.

This is how we melted the chocolate:

(label the diagram - pan, bowl, water, chocolate and heat source)

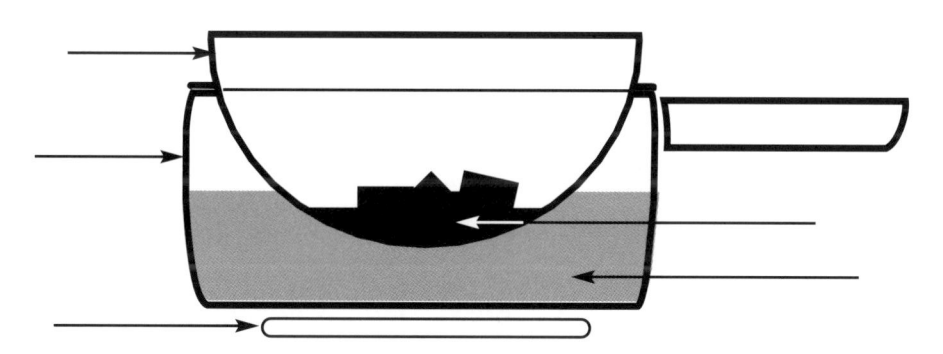

Draw what the chocolate looked like:

Before it was melted	After it was melted

Draw a picture of your completed Easter Nest and label it.

© Topical Resources. May be photocopied for classroom use only.

Five Fruit Salad

Design and Make a fruit salad to be eaten with a spoon which contains 5 fruits and a syrup/juice. It must be aesthetically pleasing.

Equipment needed:
- cutting board
- sharp knives - *used under close supervision*
- chopping board
- small bowls

Ingredients:

sugar	apples	cherries
honey	black grapes	oranges
pineapple	green grapes	lemon juice
pears	peaches	bananas
orange juice	kiwi fruit	melon

The Process:
Step 1. Photocopy the sheet opposite, one per child.
Step 2. Let the children taste all the individual fruits provided and score them using the 'faces'.
Step 3. From their recorded preferences the pupils should choose their 5 favourite.
Step 4. The pupils should carefully chop their chosen fruits into small pieces and arrange in individual bowls, 1 tablespoon of each.
Step 5. The pupils should taste the adult prepared syrups/juices: eg
lemon juice and honey
sugar melted in water
orange juice
orange juice and lemon juice
Step 6. Let the pupils select a syrup/juice and add it to their prepared fruit salad.

How the idea may be developed:
Tinned fruit salad can be compared to their made product.
Consider: Taste
Texture
Appearance
A range of fruits can be provided which the majority of pupils have not tasted before:
eg star fruits, lychees, watermelon, plums, cranberries, apricots, ugli fruit, kumquat, papaya, mango, persimmon etc.

Group fruit salads could be created in preference to the individual ones.
The countries of origin of the fruits could be researched linking the activity to the geography curriculum.

Name _____

Make a Five Fruit Salad

I have tasted all these different fruits and recorded if I liked them or I disliked them.

like   O.K.   dislike

Fruit	What I think	Chosen Fruits
	😐	
	😐	
	😐	
	😐	
	😐	
	😐	
	😐	
	😐	

I have put a ✔ in the boxes of 5 fruits that I chose to use in my Fruit Salad.

© Topical Resources. May be photocopied for classroom use only.

Layered Ice Lolly

Design and Make an ice lolly that your group will like.
Consider: Colour, taste and presentation.

Equipment needed:
- ice cube trays
- spoons
- lolly sticks
- measuring jugs
- spatulas
- ice lolly moulds
- yogurt pots

Ingredients:
- a wide variety of cordials
- food colourings
- drinking water

The Process:

Step 1. Make some ice cubes using the cordials so that the pupils can test them. The ice cubes should be made:
- using different cordials.
- using different strengths of the same cordials.

Step 2. In groups the pupils should evaluate the frozen cordials and score them using a simple system. Score them for:
- Taste
- Strength

Step 3. Record the group's preferences.

Step 4. Limit the group's choice of cordials to combine in their ice lollies.

Step 5. Look at the different shapes of containers and different sticks.

Step 6. Let the pupils decide on a shape for their lollies. Discuss the need for a mould to maintain consistency.

Step 7. Make the cordials of their chosen flavour and strength.

Step 8. Place a measured amount of the first flavour into the container and allow to freeze for 30 minutes before adding the second flavour.

Step 9. Discuss with the pupils why the first layer must be allowed 30 minutes to freeze. (Answer: If the first layer is not frozen, the the second layer will mix with it.)

Step 10. Continue adding the flavours until the lolly is formed.

Step 11. Photocopy the sheet opposite, one per child and allow the pupils time to complete the tasks.

N.B. Do not forget to place the stick or spatula into the lolly before it is frozen!

How the idea may be developed:

The pupils can add a variety of ingredients to their lollies:
eg
- small pieces of diced fruit/ tinned fruit cocktail
- Jellied sweets - eg dark coloured spiders in a light coloured lolly.

The pupils can name their lollies eg Spider Surprise etc.
How would you advertise your lolly to make people buy it?
Print your advert using a word processor.

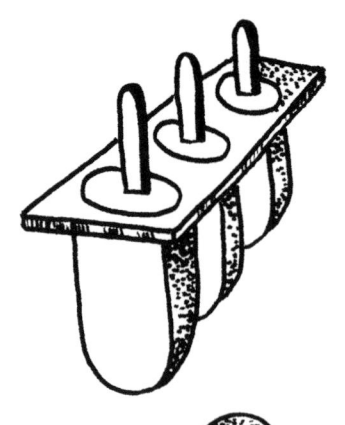

Name _____

Designing a Layered Ice Lolly

We tasted some different cordial ice cubes.

We tasted different flavours: _____ _____

_____ _____

_____ _____

We tasted different strengths:
   one part cordial to 5 parts water
   one part cordial to 4 parts water
   one part cordial to 3 parts water
   one part cordial to 2 parts water
   one part cordial to 1 parts water

We chose for our ice lolly 3 flavourings and strengths:

_____ cordial, 1 part cordial to _____ parts water.

_____ cordial, 1 part cordial to _____ parts water.

_____ cordial, 1 part cordial to _____ parts water.

This is how our finished lollies looked:

Cordial Cocktails

Design and make a cordial cocktail to their personal taste.
Link the work to a party theme eg Christmas.

Equipment needed:
- cups
- spoons
- measuring jugs
- variety of plastic glasses / containers

Ingredients:
- orange cordial
- pineapple cordial
- lime cordial
- assortment of fresh fruit juices
- sparkling water
- bottled water
- lemonade

The Process:
- Step 1. Let the pupils taste the range of cordials and mixers.
- Step 2. Photocopy the sheet opposite, one per child and record their preferences on the table using the simple scoring system.
- Step 3. Limit the pupils choices for their cocktail i.e.   1 cordial   1 mixer   1 fruit juice
  Consider: colour, taste, presentation
- Step 4. Let the pupils mix their own cocktails using spoons to measure.
- Step 5. Evaluate the finished product and make any changes required.
- Step 6. Choose a plastic glass for the final cocktail.
- Step 7. Complete the sheet by drawing and naming the finished cocktail.

How the idea may be developed:
Fruit could be added to the drinks. They should be tasted and evaluated before being added to the cocktails.
Ice cubes can be added to a summer cocktail. These can be coloured using food colourings or they can be made from the cordials and juices.

The presentation of the cocktails can be enhanced by adding:
- straws
- umbrellas
- sugar around the rim of the glass
- fruit around the rim of the glass
- a decorated mat etc.

The drinks could be sold at break times to fund the activity.

Name _____

Design and Make Cordial Cocktails

I tasted different cordials, juices and mixers and recorded my likes and dislikes.

like   O.K.   dislike

Cordials	
	😐
	😐
	😐

Fruit Juices	
	😐
	😐
	😐

Mixers	
	😐
	😐
	😐

My cocktail was made with: Cordial _____

Fruit Juice _____

Mixer _____

The colour of my cocktail was: _____

I have called my cordial cocktail:

_____

because _____

_____

My finished cocktail looked like this:

© Topical Resources. May be photocopied for classroom use only.

Flavoured Milk Shakes

Equipment needed:
- fork
- rotary whisk
- tablespoons
- plastic glasses
- hand whisk
- measuring jug
- teaspoons
- straws

Ingredients:
- Skimmed milk
- semi skimmed milk
- full fat milk
- powdered milk shake flavourings:-vanilla
  - banana
  - chocolate
  - strawberry etc.

The Process:
Step 1. In groups the children should taste the milks unflavoured. Which do they like the most? Which the least? Why?
Step 2. Record their preferences.
Step 3. Make the milk shakes using all three types of milk and allow the pupils to taste them using a teaspoon.
Step 4. Let the pupils create their own milkshakes using teaspoons to measure the powders.
Step 5. Ask which piece of equipment will the pupils use to mix the powders into the milk? Introduce the use of a fork for whisking, a hand whisk and a rotary whisk.
Step 6. Taste the milkshakes after each teaspoon of flavouring is added. Stop when the desired taste is achieved.
Step 7. Photocopy the sheet opposite, one per child and complete.

How the idea may be developed:
Ready made milk shakes can be evaluated.

Look at the ingredients on the containers of ready made milk shakes. What type of milk is used? Which milk shake do the pupils prefer, manufactured or made?

Ice cream can be added to the milk shakes. Use vanilla ice cream and ice creams that match the flavourings. The ice cream could be added in balls or whisked into the mixture. Which do the pupils prefer?

Fresh fruits can be added to the milk shakes. What will their addition do to enhance the milk shake? What problems will occur concerning the drinking of the milk shake? How can these problems be overcome?

Name _____

Make Flavoured Milkshakes

This is a labelled diagram of the ingredients of my milk shake:

We looked on the packets of the flavourings to find out what they contained. They contained:

_____ milk contains:
(type of milk chosen)

List the benefits of the nutrients in milk for the body:

Background Information for Key Stage 2 Pupils

Nutrition
Good nutrition is a matter of eating adequate but not excessive amounts of all the nutrients necessary for maintaining good health.
Many foods are a mixture of the different nutrients yet no one food is complete in itself. A balanced diet is made up of a variety of foods.
Nutrients are divided into five main groups:

      Protein, Fat, Carbohydrates, Minerals and Vitamins.

One person's requirements vary from another's and individuals can vary from day to day. If a person eats / drinks foods that provide more energy than is needed then some will be converted into body fat and the persons weight will increase.

Protein
Protein is an essential part of all living cells and provides material for growth and repair of body tissue. Proteins are made up from a combination of substances called amino acids. There are animal and plant sources of protein. More proteins are needed during periods of growth, illness and pregnancy.
Lacto vegetarians and vegans need to obtain a wide variety of proteins from plant foods as they do not eat meat and fish (vegans do not eat eggs and cheese or any dairy product).
Sources of protein include - eggs, cheese, milk, yogurt, cereals, pulses, nuts, fish and meat.

Fat
Fat provides a concentrated source of energy giving more than twice the amount of energy as that given by either proteins or carbohydrates. It is also a source of some of the essential vitamins and provides a reserve store of energy under the skin.
Fat makes an important contribution to the texture of food improving the flavour and making them more appealing.
Fat can cause weight gain if eaten in excess of the body's needs and they are a factor in heart disease where saturated fatty acids (from animals) are more dangerous than polyunsaturated acids (vegetable sources).
Sources of fat include - butter, margarine, oils, cream, cheese, nuts, chocolate, cakes, biscuits and ice cream.

Carbohydrates
Carbohydrates provide the main source of energy for bodily activities and for maintaining body temperature and are found in starches and sugars.
Sources of carbohydrates include - bread, pasta, biscuits, cakes, fruit, vegetables, sugar, potatoes and flour.
Fibre is a form of carbohydrate and is sometimes called roughage. It produces a small amount of energy because we are unable to digest it, however it adds bulk and assists the passage of food through our digestive system. Fibre is found in whole cereals, bran, fruit and vegetables.

Vitamins and Minerals
Vitamins and minerals are found in small amounts in most foods and they are essential to the body for growth, repair and general functioning of the metabolic process.
There are many vitamins and minerals which aid a wide variety of bodily functions and repairs.
Pupils could be encouraged to find as much information as they can about vitamins and the minerals Calcium, Iron, Fluorine, Sodium, Chlorine and Potassium.

Weights & Measures

Dry Measures	
Metric	Imperial
15g	½ oz
30g	1oz
60g	2oz
90g	3oz
120g	4oz (¼ lb)
150g	5oz
180g	6oz
240g	8oz (½ lb)
360g	12oz (¾ lb)
480g	16oz (1lb)

Liquid Measures		
Metric	Imperial	Spoons/Cups
15ml	½ fl oz	1 tablespoon
30ml	1 fl oz	⅛ cup
60ml	2 fl oz	¼ cup
90ml	3 fl oz	⅜ cup
125ml	4 fl oz	½ cup
150ml	5 fl oz	⅔ cup
175ml	6 fl oz	¾ cup
250ml	8 fl oz	1 cup
300ml	10 fl oz	1¼ cups
375ml	12 fl oz	1½ cups
500ml	16 fl oz	2 cups
600ml	20 fl oz	2½ cups
900ml	1½ pints	3¾ cups
1 litre	1¾ pints	4 cups (1 quart)

These conversion tables are approximate only.
The differences between the approximate and exact measurements of dry and liquid ingredients amounts to only a teaspoon or two and will not affect the result.

Oven Temperatures			
	C (Celsius)	F (Fahrenheit)	Gas Mark
very slow	120°C	250°F	1
slow	150°C	300°F	2
moderately slow	160°C	325°F	3
moderate	180°C	350°F	4
moderately hot	190°C	375°F	5
hot	200°C	400°F	6
very hot	230°C	450°F	7

© Topical Resources. May be photocopied for classroom use only.

Spiced Biscuits

Equipment needed:
- conventional oven
- mixing bowls x 2
- weighing scales
- spoons - mixing, tablespoon and teaspoon
- biscuit cutters
- baking tray
- oven gloves
- sieve
- cooling rack
- rolling pin

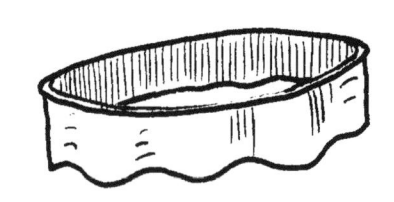

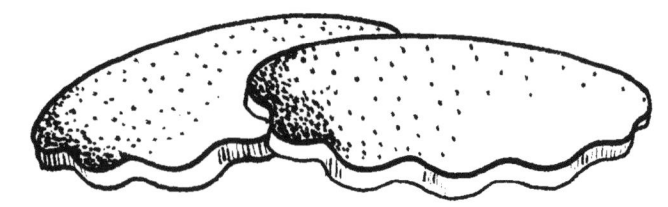

Ingredients:
- 150 grams flour
- 125 grams unsalted butter
- water as necessary
- half a teaspoon of spice 'a'
- (or 1 teaspoon of only one spice)
- half a teaspoon baking powder
- 100 grams light brown sugar
- half a teaspoon of spice 'b'

The Process:

Step 1. Provide a range of spices for the pupils to investigate by smell.
eg: ginger   cinnamon   curry   nutmeg   mixed spices

Step 2. Sieve the flour, baking powder and spices together in a mixing bowl.

Step 3. In a different larger bowl, cream the butter and sugar together.

Step 4. Add the flour mixture to the creamed sugar and margarine and mix. If the mixture is dry then add water, a teaspoon at a time, until the mixture will form a ball.

Step 5. Place the biscuit mixture onto a floured surface and roll out to approximately 4 mms thickness.

Step 6. Select the biscuit cutters required and cut them out of the dough.

Step 7. Place the biscuits onto a greased baking tray and bake in a pre-heated oven at 200 degrees celsius for 5-7 minutes or until golden brown.

Step 8. Take from the oven when cooked and transfer to a rack to cool.

Step 9. Evaluate the biscuits and score them. Record the evaluations and determine which is the favourite spiced biscuit.

Step 10. Photocopy the sheet opposite one per child and complete.

How the idea may be developed:

Before baking, almonds, currants, raisins and/or cherries could be added by pressing them into the top of the cut biscuit shapes.

N.B. If nuts are to be used then special care must be taken as to individual pupil's dietary restrictions!

Name _____

Investigate and Evaluate Spiced Biscuits

We collected words to describe the appearance of the spices:

We collected words to describe the smell of the spices:

We collected words to describe how our biscuits tasted:

My biscuits were ....
because ....
....
....

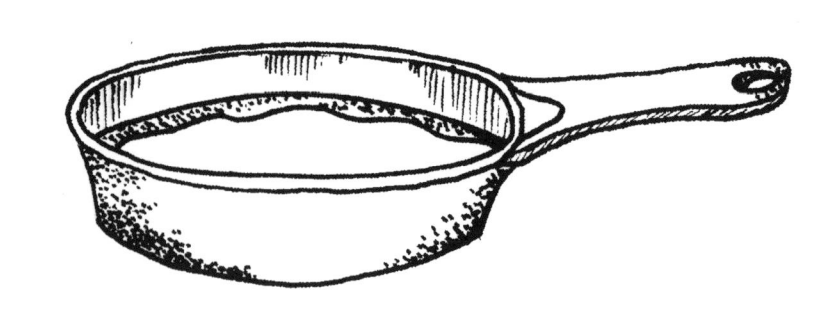

Sweet and Savoury Pancakes

Equipment needed:
- measuring jug
- mixing bowl
- fork
- hand whisk
- rotary whisk
- frying pan
- electric hob
- spatula
- spoon
- cup

Ingredients:
- 2 eggs
- 100 grams flour
- oil (or butter for frying)
- quarter of a teaspoon of salt
- 300mls milk

The Process:
Step 1. Place the eggs in a bowl and mix in the salt using either a fork, hand whisk or rotary whisk.
Step 2. Stir in the flour.
Step 3. Pour in the milk and beat the batter mixture until it resembles smooth cream adding more milk if necessary.
Step 4. Pour a small amount of oil (butter) into the frying pan and heat.
Step 5. Add one cup of the batter mixture to the oil in the pan and 'swirl' it around to cover the base of the frying pan evenly.
Step 6. Cook slowly on one side and when the batter has set, use the spatula to turn the pancake over and cook until golden brown.

How the idea may be developed:
How will you serve your Pancake?
The pupils should decide if they would prefer a sweet or savoury pancake and taste the ingredients if they are not familiar with them.

Suggested Ingredients:

lemon juice	orange juice	sugar
honey	jams	marmalade
fruits	mushrooms	beans
tomatoes	cheese etc...	

Evaluate the pancakes.
Photocopy the sheet opposite, one per child and complete.

Name _____

Investigate and Evaluate Sweet and Savoury Pancakes

You will need to use an encyclopedia and dictionaries to complete this sheet.

Pancakes are a traditional food. What does traditional mean?
_____
_____
_____

At what time of year are pancakes made?
_____

Why are pancakes made?
_____
_____
_____
_____

Write the process of how you served your pancake.
(Hint: Continue from Step 6 on opposite page)
_____
_____
_____
_____

What did you think of your pancake?
_____
_____
_____

Which pancake flavour was the favourite in your class?
_____

© Topical Resources. May be photocopied for classroom use only.

Bread and Butter Pudding

Equipment needed:
    oven proof dish
    knife
    cutting board
    fork
    mixing bowl
    oven gloves

Ingredients:
    6 thin slices of buttered stale bread cut from a loaf
    sugar
    1 handful of raisins or sultanas
    2 eggs + 1 yolk
    three quarters pint of milk
    half teaspoon vanilla essence

The Process:
Step 1.   Cut the bread and butter into triangles and remove the crusts.
Step 2.   Arrange one layer of the triangles into an ovenproof dish.
Step 3.   Sprinkle the slices with sultanas / raisins and sugar.
Step 4.   Place another layer of bread and butter triangles on top of the first.
Step 5.   Sprinkle the slices with sultanas / raisins and sugar.
Step 6.   Continue with the layers to the top of the dish.
Step 7.   Beat up the two eggs and the egg yolk and mix with the warmed milk.
Step 8.   Add the vanilla essence to the milk mixture and pour over the bread triangles in the dish.
Step 9.   Sprinkle sugar on the top and 'dot' with butter.
Step 10.   Bake the Bread and Butter pudding in an oven (150 degrees celsius) for 45 minutes - 1 hour.
Step 11.   Serve hot or cold.
Step 12.   Photocopy the sheet opposite and complete.

How the idea may be developed:
Can brown bread be used to create the pudding?
Could other dried fruits be added? The pupils may wish to try cherries or dried apricots.

Name _____

Investigate and Evaluate Bread and Butter Pudding

Circle the words that best describe:

Before Cooking

The Raisins	**Appearance**	**Feel / Texture**	**Taste**
	wrinkled	rough	sweet
	juicy	soft	soft
	squashed	dry	chewy
	shrivelled	smooth	
Add other words:	....	....	....
	....	....	....
	....	....	....

The Bread	**Appearance**	**Feel / Texture**	**Taste**
	white	dry	stale
	flat	spongy	
	juicy	rough	
Add other words:	....	....	....
	....	....	....

After Cooking

The Raisins	**Appearance**	**Feel / Texture**	**Taste**
	....	....	....
	....	....	....
	....	....	....

The Bread	**Appearance**	**Feel / Texture**	**Taste**
	....	....	....
	....	....	....
	....	....	....

Create a class list of words to describe the ingredients before and after cooking. Why has the appearance and texture changed?

Is the process reversible? _____

If not, why not?_____

_____

Meringues

Equipment needed:
- mixing bowl
- rotary whisk
- greaseproof paper
- metal spoon
- oven
- piping bag

Ingredients:
2 egg whites (size 1-2)   125 grams caster sugar

How to make the example:
Step 1.   Put the egg whites in a large bowl and whisk until stiff.
Step 2.   Whisk into the egg whites two tablespoons of the sugar.
Step 3.   Fold in the rest of the sugar with a metal spoon.
Step 4.   Spoon the mixture into a piping bag fitted with a half centimetre plain nozzle.
Step 5.   Pipe 16 rounds onto a baking tray covered with a sheet of greaseproof paper.
Step 6.   Bake in a cool oven, 120 degrees centigrade for 3 hours.
Step 7.   When the meringues are firm to the touch, remove them from the oven and leave them to cool on the baking tray.
Step 8.   Taste and evaluate the meringues.

How the idea may be developed:
How could the meringues be served?
Let the children investigate a range of fruits that could be served with the meringues and cream eg strawberries, cherries, raspberries etc..
Could the children create coloured meringues?
Could the pupils create flavoured meringues? How?

Name _____

Egg Investigations

Compare and contrast: battery farm produced eggs and free range eggs. Consider: colour, size, price, consistency of the white and the yolk of the eggs.

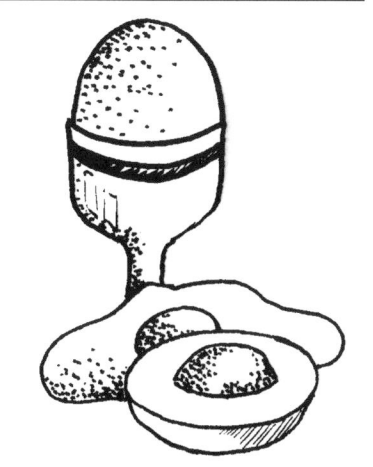

	Size	Colour	Consistency of Yolk	Consistency of White	Price
Free Range					
Battery Farm					

Research how does the lifestyle of the hens differ.

Free Range	
Battery Farm	

Discuss the different ways of cooking eggs:
List the equipment needed to cook them and illustrate what the finished product looks like.

	Boiled	Fried	Poached	Scrambled
Equipment Needed				
Finished Product				

Bread

Equipment needed:
- mixing bowl
- weighing scales
- spoon
- measuring jug
- cloth or cling film
- baking tray
- cooling tray

Ingredients:
- 240 grams flour
- 30 grams fat
- 150 ml warm water (tepid)
- 15 grams yeast
- half a teaspoon of salt

The Process:
Step 1. Place the flour and salt into a bowl and rub in the fat using your hands.
Step 2. Cream the yeast and sugar in a separate bowl and add the tepid water. Stir gently.
Step 3. Make a well in the middle of the flour mixture and pour the yeast mixture into the hole.
Step 4. Mix gently and then cover the bowl with a cloth or piece of cling film and place it in a warm place for approximately one hour until the dough has doubled in size.
Step 5. Place the dough onto a floured surface and knead gently.
Step 6. Divide the dough into 15 pieces and knead each piece into a ball.
Step 7. Gently press the balls onto a warm, greased baking tray, cover with a cloth and leave in a warm place for 30 minutes to 'prove'.
Step 8. Bake the rolls in an oven pre-heated to 230 degrees celsius for 10 - 15 minutes until golden brown and firm underneath.
Step 9. Remove from the oven when cooked and transfer to a cooling tray.
Step 10. Photocopy the sheet opposite, one per child and complete.

How the idea may be developed:
Vary the type of flour used in the recipe.
Find out why the yeast is important to the bread?
Make some bread with - half the quantity of yeast/ no yeast at all. What is the bread like?
Visit a local bakery or supermarket and look at as wide a range of breads as possible.
Taste and evaluate as wide a range of breads as is possible.
Carry out a survey of the pupils in your class. What sort of bread do they eat at home?
eg white sliced, white unsliced, brown sliced, brown unsliced, wholemeal etc..

Name _____

How to Make Bread

Use pictures and / or words to describe the process in as much detail as possible so that other pupils could follow your instructions.

Equipment needed	Ingredients
Step 1	Step 2
Step 3	Step 4
Step 5	Step 6

Chapatti

(Wholewheat Unleavened Bread)

Because of the process involved, this activity should be carried out with small groups and adult supervision is essential. It may be appropriate for an adult to carry out the cooking activities and for the pupils to record the process.

Equipment needed:
- weighing scales
- sieve
- rolling pin
- saucepan
- mixing bowl

Ingredients:
- 275g wholemeal flour
- 175ml hot water
- half a teaspoon salt
- 2 tablespoons oil

The Process:

Step 1. Sieve the flour and salt into a mixing bowl, add the oil and add enough water in small amounts until a soft dough is made.

Step 2. Knead the mixture on a floured surface for 10 minutes until it is no longer sticky.

Step 3. Cover the bowl and leave for 1 hour.

Step 4. Divide the mixture into 14 balls and flatten each ball.

Step 5. Using a rolling pin, roll out each ball to a circle of about 15cm diameter on a floured surface.

Step 6. Heat a frying pan over a medium heat and place a chapatti into it. Cook the chapatti for 2 minutes on one side - until brown spots appear - and then turn the chapatti over and cook the other side. Do not place any oil into the frying pan as chapattis are cooked dry.

Step 7. Take the chapatti and place under a very hot pre-heated grill for a few seconds and it will 'puff up'.

Step 8. Turn the chapatti over and cook the other side until that too 'puffs up'.

Step 9. Brush the cooked chapattis with ghee and pile up keeping warm whilst the others are cooked.

To create ghee, photocopy the opposite sheet and follow the instructions.

How the idea may be developed:

The chapattis can be served with a variety of curries and dips. The pupils can create the dishes to accompany the chappatis.

Name _____

Ghee - Clarified Butter

Ghee can be stored in an airtight bottle in a cool place.
List the equipment and ingredients used to create the ghee and record the process by drawing pictures.

Equipment needed:	Ingredients:
Step 1 Heat 225g of butter in a saucepan over a low heat.	Step 2 Let it simmer for 15 - 20 minutes.
Step 3 Wait until all the white residue has turned brown.	Step 4 Remove from the heat.
Step 5 Strain the butter and allow to cool.	Step 6 Pour into an airtight container.

Pizza Base

Equipment needed:
- sieve
- large bowl
- mixing spoon
- cloth / cling film
- rolling pin
- baking tray
- oven

Ingredients:
- 375 grams strong white flour
- one and a half teaspoons of salt
- 1 sachet of easy blend yeast
- 1 tablespoon extra virgin olive oil
- 220 mls warm water

The Process:

Step 1. Sieve the salt, yeast and flour into a large bowl and mix together.
Step 2. Make a hole in the middle of the mixture and pour all of the warm water in. Stir the mixture until it forms a soft dough.
Step 3. Place the dough onto a floured surface and knead for 10 - 15 minutes until it feels smooth and springy.
Step 4. Place the dough into a clean, lightly oiled bowl and cover the bowl with either a cloth or a piece of cling film.
Step 5. Place the covered bowl in a warm place for 2 hours until the dough has doubled in size.
Step 6. Divide the dough into 4 pieces and roll out the pizza dough on a floured surface to create 4 bases measuring approximately 20cms.
Step 7. Place the bases on a floured baking tray and cook in an oven heated to 240 degrees celsius for 5 - 10 minutes, do not allow them to go brown.
Step 8. Add toppings.
Step 9. Photocopy the sheet opposite, one per child and complete.

How the idea may be developed
Use wholemeal flour instead of white flour.
Make smaller pizza bases and use a biscuit cutter to cut them from the dough.
Make large pizza bases and divide them into quarters to place 4 different toppings on each pizza.

Name _____

How to Make a Pizza Base

Use pictures and / or words to describe the process in as much detail as possible so that other pupils could create your pizza.

Equipment needed	Ingredients
Step 1	Step 2
Step 3	Step 4
Step 5	Step 6

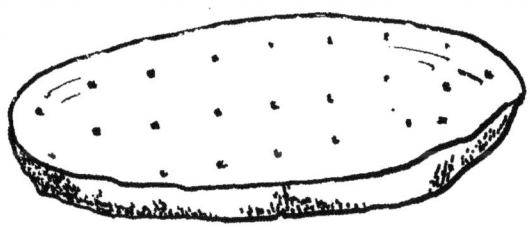

Pizza Topping

Equipment needed:
    blunt knives for spreading
    sharp knives for cutting
    spoons
    mixing bowls
    grater
    oven gloves

Ingredients:
    canned tomatoes chopped and whole
    a variety of cheeses
    tomato puree
    herbs
    bacon (cooked)
    sausages (cooked)
    onions (cooked)
    peppers (cooked)
    as wide a variety of cooked vegetables as possible.

The Process:

Step 1.   All of the ingredients which are available for toppings should be available to the pupils so that they can make choices.

Step 2.   Collect pictures of pizzas from magazines and manufactured pizza packaging to help with the pupils designing.

Step 3.   Photocopy the sheet opposite, one per child and allow time for them to complete their design.

Step 4.   Each pupil should arrange the topping on their pizza base and then it should be placed in the oven to cook for 10 - 15 minutes on a floured baking tray at a temperature of 240 degrees celsius.

Step 5.   When cooked care should be taken when removing the pizza from the oven as it will be very hot. Always use oven gloves.

Step 6.   Let the pupils eat their pizzas whilst hot and evaluate.

Step 7.   Discuss their findings and any changes they would make. It is not necessary to remake the pizza, verbal evaluation is sufficient.

How the idea may be developed:

If the pizza toppings are the activity and tasting activities are involved then bought pizza bases or packet pizza base mixes can be used.
The toppings could be placed onto toasted finger rolls or pieces of french stick.

Name _____

My Pizza Design

Fill in the key

Colour							
Ingredient							

I liked my pizza because:
_____

It could be improved by
_____

Jacket Potato

Equipment needed:
- mixing bowls
- spoons
- sharp knife for cutting
- baking tray
- fork
- paper towels
- grater
- plate
- chopping board
- conventional oven
- microwave oven (optional)

Ingredients:
- cheese
- pepper
- baked beans
- sausages(cooked)
- potatoes
- onions (cooked)
- sweetcorn
- salt
- bacon(cooked)
- mushrooms (cooked)

The Process:

Step 1. Photocopy the sheet opposite, one per child and allow time for the children to discuss and draw their designs.

Step 2. All of the ingredients should be available to the pupils so that they can make choices.

Step 3. Wash one medium sized potato for each child.

Step 4. Dry the potatoes and prick them with a fork. This will help the potatoes cook in a shorter time.

Step 5. Cook the potatoes in a conventional oven for 25 minutes at a temperature of 230 degrees celsius or in a microwave at the highest setting for 4 minutes.

Step 6. Remove the potatoes and check that they are soft (cooked). If they are not, return them to the heat source until they are cooked.

Step 7. Hold the potatoes with a paper towel and take care. They will be very hot!
Cut the potatoes in half and scoop out the middle into a mixing bowl.

Step 8. Add the ingredients that the pupils have chosen but ensure that:
- cheese has been grated
- vegetables have been diced and cooked
- all ingredients are chopped

Step 9. Mix the ingredients together and put them back into the skins which should then be placed on a baking tray and cooked in a conventional oven for a further 10 minutes. (or in a microwave for 2 minutes)

Step 10. Eat the jacket potatoes whilst hot and evaluate. Because each child has two halves, the pupils could evaluate each others recipes.

Name _____

Design and Make a Tasty Jacket Potato

I have chosen the following ingredients to mix with the potatoes:

_____
_____
_____
_____

Here is an annotated (labelled) drawing of my jacket potato.

These words describe the taste, the appearance and the texture of my jacket potato:

Taste	Appearance	Texture

Flavoured Omelette

Equipment needed:
- knife
- cutting board
- frying pan
- whisk
- mixing bowl
- serving plate

Ingredients:
- 3 tablespoons olive oil
- 3 cloves crushed garlic
- 4 eggs
- 2 large potatoes boiled and chopped
- 2 table spoons chopped parsley
- 2 chopped onions
- 1 red pepper, cored and chopped
- salt + pepper

The Process:
Step 1. Heat 2 table spoons of olive oil in a frying pan and add the onions; cook until soft.
Step 2. Add the garlic and red pepper and cook slowly on a low heat for approximately 8 minutes.
Step 3. Whisk the eggs with salt and pepper to taste in a large mixing bowl.
Step 4. Stir in the potatoes and parsley.
Step 5. Add the fried onions, garlic and peppers.
Step 6. Heat the remaining oil in a frying pan and pour in the omelette mixture making sure it is spread evenly over the base of the frying pan.
Step 7. Cook the omelette for 5 minutes over a low light, shaking the pan to prevent the omelette sticking.
Step 8. Place the pan under a pre heated moderate grill for 3 minutes to cook the top of the omelette.
Step 9. Slide the omelette onto a warm serving plate and cut into wedges to serve.
Step 10. Photocopy the sheet opposite and complete.

How the idea may be developed:
Grated cheese can be added to the top of the omelette and melted under the grill.
The omelette could be served cold.

The mixture can be divided to create smaller omelettes which can be turned over to cook both sides. If the mixture is divided then the pupils can add other ingredients eg cooked sausages, green peppers, cooked bacon, mushrooms etc.

Name _____

Design and Make a Flavoured Omelette

We all created a basic omelette mixture in groups and then added additional ingredients to create our own omelettes.

How we created the basic mixture:

....
....
....
....
....

Additional Ingredients:

1. ....
2. ....
3. ....
4. ....
5. ....

Evaluation.

We tasted our omelettes and I thought that mine was:

....
....
....
....
....

This is an annotated drawing of my finished omelette:

© Topical Resources. May be photocopied for classroom use only.

Individual Decorated Christmas Cake

Equipment needed:
- conventional oven
- greaseproof paper
- mixing bowls
- sterilised small tins
- grater
- fork
- mixing spoons

Ingredients:
- 100 grams self raising flour
- 100 grams barbados sugar
- 1 tablespoon syrup (treacle)
- 200 grams currants
- 100 grams raisins
- 25 grams peel
- 100 grams butter
- 1 and a half eggs
- quarter of a teaspoon mixed spice
- 100 grams sultanas
- 25 grams almonds
- 50 grams cherries
- half the rind and the juice of- 1 orange, 1 lemon, 1 lime

The Process:
- Step 1. Grease the small sterilised tins. Small baked bean tins or similar sized containers are the most suitable.
- Step 2. Line the tins with greaseproof paper along the base and up the sides so that the paper sticks up over the edge of the tin.
- Step 3. Grease the paper.
- Step 4. Cream the butter and sugar together in a large bowl.
- Step 5. Beat the eggs and the rind in a different bowl and then add them to the creamed ingredients.
- Step 6. Add the fruit, nuts and peel and mix.
- Step 7. Fold into the mixture the flour, spices, treacle and juices.
- Step 8. Spoon the mixture into the tins. It will make approximately 20 small cakes.
- Step 9. Level the top of the mixture in the tins and place a circle of greaseproof paper on the top which has been cut to the size of the tin.
- Step 10. Bake in a pre-heated oven at 150 degrees celsius for approximately 50 minutes. Test that the cake is cooked by pressing gently on the top, if the cake is cooked the top should spring back when pressed.
- Step 11. Remove from the oven and allow to cool, remove from the tin.
- Step 12. When the cake is cold it should be covered in ready mixed almond paste and then iced adding decoration to the top whilst the icing is wet eg cherries, nuts etc...
- Step 13. Photocopy the sheet opposite and allow the pupils to decorate the scene that they would like to wrap around the outside edge of the cake.

How the idea may be developed:
The pupils could select their own ingredients to add to the cake after evaluating them.
Two cakes could be made by each pupil so that one could be sold to fund the activity?
The pupils imaginations should be given time to flourish when decorating their cake
eg coloured icing, figures, greetings, packaging etc.

Name _____

Design a Christmas Cake Decoration

Decorate a given design or create your own pattern.

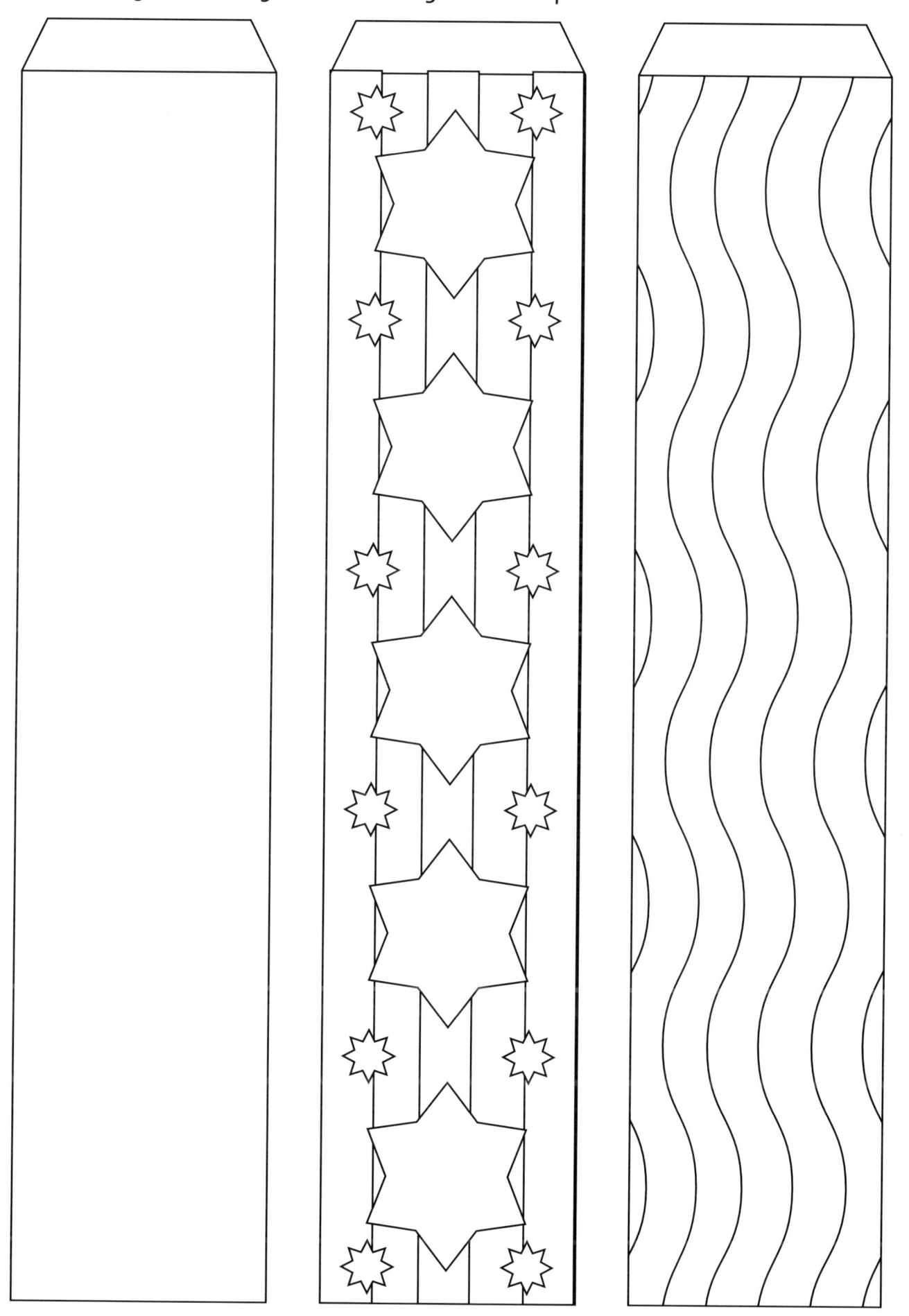

© Topical Resources. May be photocopied for classroom use only.

57

Additional Recipes

Vegetable Soup

Equipment needed:
- large saucepan
- sharp knife
- chopping board
- sieve
- electric hob

Ingredients:
- 50 grams butter
- 1 onion
- 2 carrots
- 2 celery sticks
- 2 medium potatoes
- 1 can chopped tomatoes
- 600 ml vegetable stock
- 1 teaspoon tomato puree
- salt & pepper

The Process:
- Step 1. Melt the butter in a large pan.
- Step 2. Chop the vegetables into small pieces and add them to the pan cooking them until they are soft.
- Step 3. Add the tin of chopped tomatoes and their juice to the pan.
- Step 4. Add the stock and tomato puree to the pan and heat.
- Step 5. Taste the soup and add the salt and pepper as necessary.
- Step 6. Bring the soup to the boil, cover and simmer for 30 minutes.
- Step 7. Remove the soup from the heat and allow to cool. When cool strain the soup through the sieve by rubbing.
- Step 8. Return the soup to the heat and bring to the boil.
- Step 9. Check the seasoning, serve and evaluate. Consider:
    - taste, appearance, texture.
- Step 10. Photocopy the sheet opposite, one per child and complete.

How the idea may be developed:

Compare the made vegetable soup with manufactured vegetable soup in:
- a packet
- a tin

Create a menu which contains a soup as a starter.

Create a vegetable soup with a wider variety of ingredients.
Make a list of the different types of soups that are featured in recipe books.

Spiced Beans

Equipment needed:
- frying pan
- spatula
- strainer
- knives

Ingredients:
- 425g can red kidney beans
- 3 tbs cooking oil
- 1 teaspoon carom seeds
- 1 large onion chopped
- 2 cloves garlic crushed
- 1 and a half tsp salt
- 1 tsp chilli powder
- 1 tsp ground turmeric
- 3 tbs ground coriander
- 1 large tin chopped tomatoes
- 2 tsp granulated sugar

The Process:
- Step 1. Heat the oil in a frying pan or a pan and add the carom seeds, allow them to sizzle.
- Step 2. Add the onions and cook for 2 minutes.
- Step 3. Add the salt, chilli, turmeric, and ground coriander; stir fry for 1 minute.
- Step 4. Add the tomatoes, garlic and sugar and simmer for 5 minutes.
- Step 5. Strain and wash the kidney beans and add to the pan.
- Step 6. Stir the beans and add water to the mixture if needed.

How the idea may be developed:

Other beans could be used as a basis for the recipe; try baked beans or butter beans.

Other spices could be used. Tests would have to be carried out for the pupils to choose which spices they wanted, they would have to smell the spices.

What could the spiced beans be served with? Try rice, spaghetti, jacket potatoes.

Additional Recipes

Vegetable Kebabs

Equipment needed:
- knives
- frying pan
- saucepan
- skewers
- baking foil
- kitchen paper
- oven gloves

Ingredients:
- 245g courgettes - sliced to 3cm cubes
- 225g courgettes - sliced to 3cm cubes
- salt
- 10 tablespoons olive / sunflower oil
- half a teaspoon ground cumin
- 125g cauliflower florets
- 125g onion - sliced to 3cm cubes
- 125g mushrooms - whole
- 75g green peppers - sliced
- 2 tomatoes - halved
- 2 slices wholemeal bread cut into 3cm cubes
- fresh ground black pepper

The Process:
Step 1. Fry the onions, mushrooms and bread cubes slowly in oil until they colour.
Step 2. Remove them from the heat and drain off the oil on kitchen paper.
Step 3. Boil the courgettes, cauliflower florets and aubergines until soft, remove them from the heat and allow to cool.
Step 4. Arrange the ingredients on skewers, alternating the ingredients.
Step 5. Mix the cumin with the oil.
Step 6. Place single kebabs onto kitchen foil, pour a little of the oil mixture over them and add salt and pepper to taste. Wrap the foil around the kebab to form a parcel.
Step 7. Cook the parcels in a pre heated moderately hot oven for 15 - 20 minutes.

How the idea may be developed:
Barbecue the kebabs.
Add sausages, pineapple cubes, pieces of beef burger.
Could fruit kebabs be created? What 'juices' would you cook them in?

Vegetable Risotto

Equipment needed:
- knives
- saucepan
- spatula
- spoon
- frying pan

Ingredients:
- 4 tablespoons oil
- 175g brown rice
- 600ml water
- 1 chopped onion
- 3 cloves crushed garlic
- 1 tsp salt
- 1 red pepper, cored, seeded and chopped
- 250g button mushrooms, sliced
- 1 x 425 can of red kidney beans
- 3 tbs chopped parsley
- 1 tbsp soya sauce
- 50g roasted cashew nuts

The Process:
Step 1. Heat 2 tablespoons of oil in a saucepan and add the chopped onions, frying until soft.
Step 2. To the pan add the rice and the garlic and cook for 2 minutes stirring constantly.
Step 3. Add the water and salt and bring to the boil, stirring all the time.
Step 4. Cover the pan and simmer for approximately 35 - 40 minutes until all the water is absorbed.
Step 5. Heat the remaining oil in a frying pan and fry the peppers for 5 minutes.
Step 6. Add the mushrooms and fry for 3 minutes.
Step 7. Add the cooked rice, kidney beans, parsley, nuts and soya sauce and mix thoroughly.
Step 8. Cook the risotto until all the beans and ingredients are heated through.

How the idea may be developed:
Different types of beans could be used instead of the red kidney beans or a variety of beans could be added to the recipe. Try baked beans, green beans, butter beans etc.

The pupils could choose different types of vegetables to add to the risotto - celery, potatoes, peas, green and yellow peppers etc.

Could the rice be coloured? This would be suitable for a festival food or food for a celebration.

Additional Recipes

Vegetable Curry

Equipment needed:
- knives
- saucepan
- chopping board
- spoons

Ingredients:
- 5 tbs cooking oil
- 2 tbs ground coriander
- 3 black peppercorns - crushed
- 1 tsp chilli powder
- 1 large onion - chopped
- 1 large potato
- 1 large tin chopped tomatoes
- 2 medium sized carrots
- 2 tbs tomato puree
- 2 cups hot water
- 1 teaspoon sea salt
- 125g frozen peas
- 1 teaspoon ground turmeric

The Process:
- Step 1. Fry the chopped onion and crushed black peppercorns slowly in oil for 5 minutes.
- Step 2. Add the tinned tomatoes and cook for 2 minutes.
- Step 3. Add the tomato puree, salt, ground coriander, turmeric and chilli powder and cook for 3 minutes.
- Step 4. Cut the potato and carrots into small cubes and add to the pan. Cook for 10 minutes.
- Step 5. Add the water and cook for a further 10 minutes.
- Step 6. Add the peas and cook until they are heated through, approximately 5 minutes.

How the idea may be developed:
Test a variety of spices that could be added to your curry to give it more / a different flavour. Try cinnamon, cardamom pods, paprika.

Look at the ingredients on a packet / tin of ready made curry powder, list the ingredients.
Where do the spices come from? Use a large scale world map and mark the countries of origin.

Use a variety of extra / alternative vegetables - cauliflower, mushrooms, red and green peppers etc...
Could hard boiled eggs be added to the curry prior to serving?

Test manufactured curries. Look at the ingredients used. Create an Indian feast and make chapattis, curries and samosas.
Research festivals and celebration

Vegetable Samosas Pastry

Equipment needed:
- sieve
- mixing bowl
- flour dredger
- frying pan
- clean tea towel

Ingredients:
- 500g plain flour
- 1 tsp salt; 1 tsp oil; 1 tsp lemon juice
- cold water
- 10 - 12 tbs oil for brushing
- oil for frying

The Process:
- Step 1. Sift the flour and salt into a mixing bowl and rub in the oil, lemon juice and enough water to bind the mixture into a dough.
- Step 2. Divide the dough into small pieces - about walnut size.
- Step 3. Flatten each piece and roll out on a floured surface until they become about 8cm in diameter. Repeat the process until all the dough has been used.
- Step 4. Brush each disc with oil and sprinkle with flour using a flour dredger.
- Step 5. Pair up the discs with the oiled and floured sides together and using a rolling pin roll out the discs until they become as thin as possible whilst still retaining their circular shape.
- Step 6. Heat a small amount of oil in a frying pan and cook the discs in their pairs turning them over as soon as little bubbles appear.
- Step 7. Separate the 2 discs carefully and stack with the bubble sides down. Do not over cook!
- Step 8. To keep the discs soft, wrap the stack in a clean tea towel.

How to create the samosas using the dough discs and the filling:
Take 1 disc and cut off the edges (as in the diagram).
to make two parcels.
Cut the strip down the middle.
Use flour and water paste to fold up from the line AB to create the base of the samosa.

Fold B to C to create an envelope.
Fill the envelope with the cold filling and fold over the flap sticking in place with the flour and water paste.
Cut off the surplus. Make all the samosas and deep fry them on a medium heat until they are golden brown. Serve the samosas either hot or cold.

Additional Recipes

Vegetable Samosas Filling

Equipment needed:
- knives
- chopping board
- frying pan
- spoons

Ingredients:
- 1 large onion - chopped
- 1 large potato - diced
- 3 carrots - diced
- 120g frozen peas
- 8 tbs cooking oil
- 1 tsp mustard seeds
- 1 tsp cumin seeds
- 1 tsp turmeric
- 1 tsp salt
- 1 tsp chilli powder
- 2tbs ground coriander
- 1 tsp granulated sugar
- 2 tbs sesame seeds
- juice of 1 lemon

The Process:
- Step 1. Peel and chop the onion into small pieces.
- Step 2. Peel the potatoes and carrots and cut them into small cubes.
- Step 3. Defrost the peas.
- Step 4. Heat the oil in a frying pan and add the mustard seeds and cumin seeds. Cook the seeds until the 'popping' stops.
- Step 5. Add the onions to the pan and cook for 1 minute.
- Step 6. Add the carrots, potatoes, salt and turmeric and cook for 5 minutes.
- Step 7. Add the peas and cook until tender.
- Step 8. Add the chilli powder, sugar and ground coriander and cook for 2 minutes.
- Step 9. Add the sesame seeds and lemon juice and cook for a further 1 minute.
- Step 10. Allow to cool before placing into the cases made with the pastry.

How the idea may be developed:

Test a variety of spices that could be added to your samosa to give it more / a different flavour. Try cinnamon, cardamom pods, paprika.

Use a variety of extra / alternative vegetables - cauliflower, mushrooms, red and green peppers etc... Write a list of words that describe the taste of you samosa. Compare your samosa to bought manufactured samosas. Which do you prefer. Calculate how much your samosas have cost to make each and compare the price to that of shop bought samosas. Discuss your findings.

Basic Recipes:

Biscuits

Ingredients:
- 100 grams butter (or margarine)
- 100 grams caster sugar
- 200 grams plain flour
- 1 egg
- milk as needed

Process:
- Step 1. Put the flour into a large mixing bowl.
- Step 2. Place the sugar and butter in a bowl and cream together.
- Step 3. Beat the egg in a cup.
- Step 4. Add the creamed mixture and the egg to the flour and mix well.
- Step 5. Roll out the biscuit mixture on a floured surface and cut out the required shapes.
- Step 6. Bake the biscuits in a pre-heated oven at 180 degrees centigrade for approximately 20 minutes or until golden brown.
- Step 7. Remove from the oven and allow to cool on a cooling rack.

Add 1 teaspoon of spices to the above mixture to create spice biscuits.
Add 1 tablespoon of cocoa to the above mixture for cocoa biscuits.
Replace 100 grams of the flour with 100 grams of oatmeal and double the fat content to make Oatmeal Shortie Biscuits.

Buns

Ingredients:
- 100 grams butter / margarine
- 1 large egg
- 100 grams self raising flour
- 100 grams caster sugar
- 3 tablespoons milk / water

Process:
- Step 1. Cream together the butter and sugar.
- Step 2. Beat the egg and add to the mixture.
- Step 3. Fold the flour into the mixture.
- Step 4. Spoon the mixture into 15 paper bun cases in a bun tin and place in a pre-heated oven at 200 degrees centigrade for 10 - 12 minutes until brown.
- Step 5. Remove from the oven and allow to cool.

Food Packaging - Pillow pack

Cut along the black lines.
Fold along the dotted lines.

Stick the glued tab under here

Cut out this section if you want a window in your packaging

glue along here

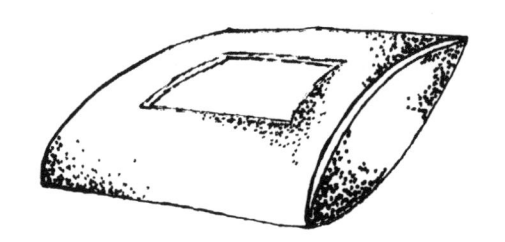

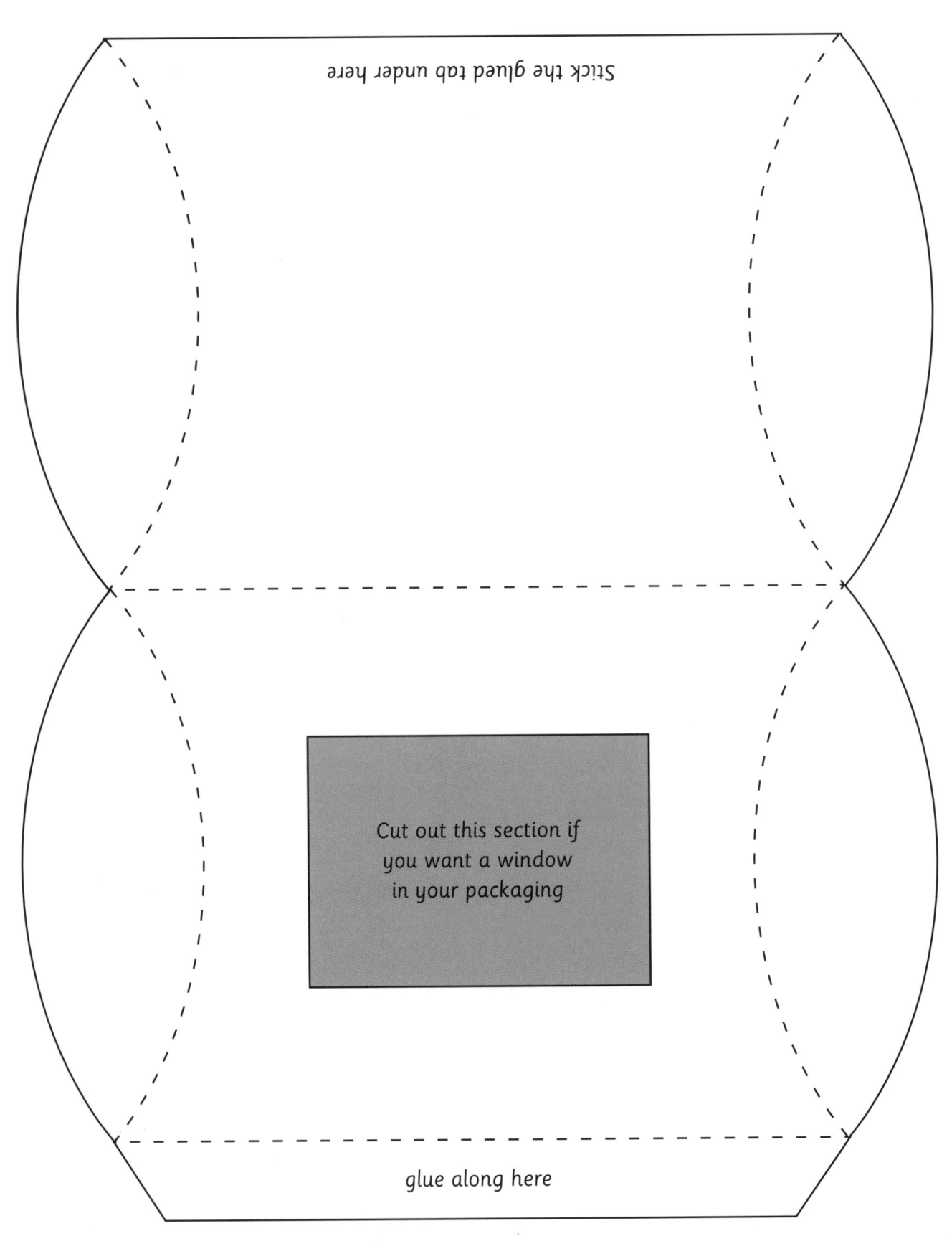

Photocopy the sheet, one per child. Let the pupils decorate the reverse side of the photocopy using pencil crayons or felt tips. The photocopy can be pasted onto thicker card to create a stronger package. A window could be cut out to display the food items.

Food Packaging - Box With Window

Cut along the black lines.
Fold along the dotted lines.

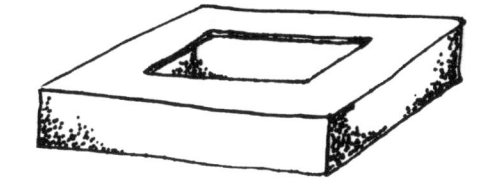

glue along here

tab

tab

Cut out this section if you want a window in your packaging

Let the pupils investigate and disassemble some manufactured packaging before this activity takes place to show them how the structures are made.

Stick the glued tab under here

Food Packaging - Paper Carrier Bag

Cut along the black lines. Fold along the dotted lines.

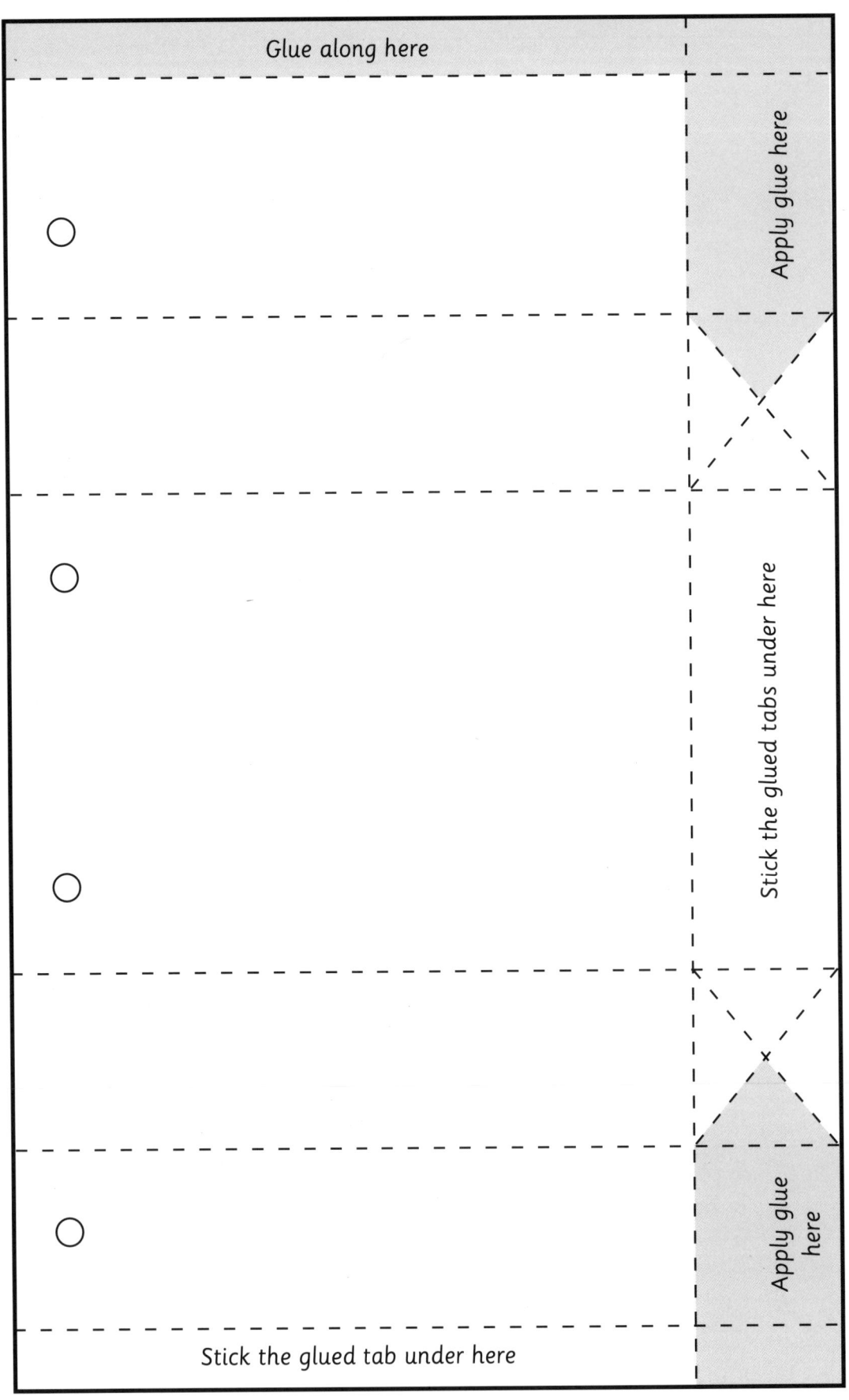

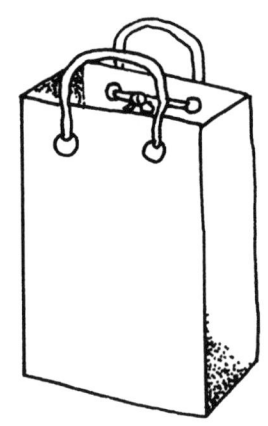

Glue along here

Apply glue here

Stick the glued tabs under here

Apply glue here

Stick the glued tab under here

Let the pupils create their own designs or cover with wrapping paper. Use cord or ribbon to form handles.

© Topical Resources. May be photocopied for classroom use only.